THE PSYCHOLOGY OF SAILING

For Dinghies and Keelboats

Dedication

With thanks to Professor Ian Maynard of Sheffield Hallam University, Tim Powell from Sales Academy Ltd and Sarah Norbury.

IAN BROWN

THE PSYCHOLOGY OF SAILING

For Dinghies and Keelboats

Adlard Coles Nautical
London

Published by
an imprint o
36 Soho Squ
www.adlardc

Copyright © Ian Brown 2010

Photographs on pages iii, v, 3, 11, 14, 27, 31, 35, 37, 39, 45, 47, 51, 58, 65, 68, 71, 78, 86, 91, 95, 100, 105, 111, 115, 118 © Eddie Mays 2010

First edition published 2010

ISBN 978-1-4081-2447-5

A CIP catalogue record for this book is available from the British Library.

This book is produced using paper that is made from wood grown in managed, sustainable forests. It is natural, renewable and recyclable. The logging and manufacturing processes conform to the environmental regulations of the country of origin.

Typeset in 10/12.5pt pt Caslon 540 by Palimpsest Book Production Limited, Grangemouth, Stirlingshire
Printed and bound in Spain by GraphyCems

Note: while all reasonable care has been taken in the publication of this book, the publisher takes no responsibility for the use of the methods or products described in the book.

Contents

Preface

I have had an interest in sport psychology since 1983 when, as a competitor at a world sailing championship, I witnessed the complete and utter self-destruction of the red hot favourite. The competitor in question had a mediocre result in the first race. Later that afternoon he and his crew member were seen cutting slits into the back of their mast with a hacksaw to try to make it bend in a different way. The next day they had another average result after which they started re-cutting the luff curve on their mainsail. After yet another poor result in race three the pair were seen in the dinghy park throwing bits of the boat at each other: rudder, centreboard and spinnaker pole all received the same treatment before they eventually packed up their boat and headed home.

I looked on in disbelief, absolutely astonished at what pressure and expectation had done to this very talented sailor. Sport psychology was virtually unheard of at the time so later that year I started a degree in mainstream psychology in the hope of developing an understanding of how the mind can interact with performance and how that might be applied to sport. Fortunately one of my tutors not only had an interest in the developing field of sport psychology but was also a keen sailor. This combination meant that I could conduct my undergraduate research in an area of psychology that wasn't considered mainstream at the time.

After I graduated my life took me in a different direction, although as a competitive sailor I maintained an interest in what was happening in the world of sport psychology. Fast forward a dozen years or so and the time was right for me to go back to school and in 1999 I began a masters degree in sport psychology. With my background in sailing and with the help of one of my tutors, Professor Ian Maynard, I began working as one of several sport psychologists contracted to the RYA on a part time basis. In this role I worked with several of the youth squads as well as the Olympic development squads and consider myself privileged to have worked with several sailors who went on to win Olympic medals and achieve significant successes on the World stage.

Incidentally, although I don't remember his name, I do know that the sailor who lost his head in 1983 did regain his composure, went on to achieve great things within the sport and was last seen sailing aboard an America's Cup contender!

Ian Brown, BSc, MSc, CPsychol

What is sport psychology and why do we need it?

> ❝ We are what we repeatedly do.
> Excellence is not an act but a habit... ❞
> **Aristotle**

Although there are references as far back in time as the ancient Greeks regarding the importance of mental skills for success in competition, sport psychology is actually a relatively new discipline, having only really become mainstream since the mid 1980s. Since then an ever increasing number of sportsmen and sportswomen across the full spectrum of sports have seen performance benefits from formally introducing sport psychology into their programmes. However, for many people sport psychology is something of a dark art, a mystery shrouded in myth and fiction. This book aims to dispel some of the myths by explaining what sport psychology actually is, and how it can be applied to sailing. The book provides practical advice based upon the application of current research and best practice as identified by many top sailors, and should be useful to any competitive sailor whether they are club level or Olympic aspirants.

Opposite page: There is a clear relationship between thought, emotions and performance

There is no doubt that there is a clear relationship between how a sportsperson harnesses and uses their thoughts and emotions and their subsequent physical performance. Evidence of this relationship can be readily found in academic literature and the media. Both are littered with quotes such as:

'The dividing line between good performers and great performers often comes down to mental toughness.'

'In most instances talent and hard work provide no guarantee of success; athletes must have control of their mind.'

It is fair to say that the majority of men and women across all sports acknowledge that a significant part of their overall success is determined by what is going on inside

their heads – *what* they think and *how* they think – and that they regard this as important as developing their technique and fitness. Crucially this applies to both training and competition. Sailing is no exception. In fact it is widely accepted among top sailors that the rather unique aspects of the sport place a premium on having well refined and well rehearsed mental skills. Sailing is widely regarded as being amongst the most highly complex and technical sports, certainly right up there alongside the likes of Formula 1. It requires a high degree of physical and mental agility with success often being dependent upon the sailor's ability to rapidly analyse a multitude of complicated and often conflicting data. The raw components of sailing – the wind and the waves – are not controllable and are different every time you go afloat. In addition, the 'playing surface' is very large and often very unpredictable making it impossible to cover all the bases; you never quite know what the other competitors are going to do or what might happen next. Combine this with the fact that going to a major regatta may require the sailor to be fully focused for anything up to ten days, and it becomes easy to see the importance of being mentally strong.

Britain's greatest ever Olympian, Sir Steve Redgrave, once said that the least well developed part of most sportspeople is their brains. He wasn't saying that they are poorly educated or inherently lacking in the grey matter department, but he was suggesting that many sportspeople spend a lot of time and effort developing their physical and technical skills, but not so much time working on their mental skills. He *was* saying that it is relatively easy to improve physically and technically (much of the time it is just a question of application and hard work) but because it is easy for one person it is easy for everyone. He went on to say that when the going gets tough it is mental skills that provide the competitive edge.

Putting this another way, as you reach the higher levels of any sport, the physical and technical skills of the performers become more equalised and it therefore becomes ever more difficult to obtain any sort of a performance edge. In a sailing context what this means is that at the elite level all of the sailors will be fit and well nourished, every boat will be prepared impeccably, everybody will have the most appropriate kit, sails and rigs, everybody's boat handling will be as near to perfect as it can be and nothing will be left to chance. At the highest levels of the sport therefore the physical and technical skills across the top performers arguably become less of a differentiator than what is happening inside their heads. As the physical and technical capabilities of the performers become more equal, the mental aspect becomes more critical. At the elite level, the difference between those sailors that actually have the ability to win, and those that just *think* that they have the ability to win is often largely down to mental preparation and mental toughness. When Ben Ainslie won his gold medal at the Athens Olympics, he was probably the first to admit that the regatta was won on more than just boatspeed and technical abilities. The regatta was largely sailed in light to moderate shifty winds, and although boatspeed and technique are important for any regatta it was Ben's incredible mental strengths that saw him come through so strongly, especially after being disqualified in a race early on in the regatta.

Having well rehearsed mental skills and the ability to use them effectively is not the exclusive domain of the elite. Although these skills will often be the difference between success and failure at the highest levels, the reality is that they have the potential to make a difference to any sportsperson, regardless of the level at which they are competing. In fact many top performers acknowledge that they could perhaps have been performing at higher levels earlier had they had access to sport psychology at earlier stages in their sporting careers. In any sport youngsters are encouraged to begin systematically developing their physical and technical skills from a young age and there is no real reason why mental skills should be any different.

The fundamental aim of sport psychology therefore is to help sports performers to develop a set of skills that help to control what goes on inside their heads, i.e. their thoughts and emotions, so that they can perform at their best even when the pressure is really on. This means being able to control thoughts and emotions to the degree that anything recognised as being unwanted, unhelpful or disruptive is either pushed to one side or replaced with something more appropriate or positive. Of course this is sometimes easier said than done; developing an awareness of what a problem might be or where it might lie is not always straightforward. However, what many people don't appreciate, whether they are the performers themselves, their coaches, parents or anybody else is that sport psychology is by no means solely about helping people to overcome problems or difficulties. Problem solving is certainly an integral facet of sport psychology but for most people sport psychology is about performance enhancement through the development of a personal mental 'tool box' that complements the physical and technical skills that most performers strive for.

Many of the techniques used by sports psychologists have come from watching successful performers and seeing how they cope with the pressure of competition and how they approach their training sessions. So if you begin to read this book and think that sport psychology is really just common sense, then you wouldn't be far from the truth. Sport psychology isn't anything magical or mystical, it just aims to help you to develop a set of mental skills which will help you to perform at your best more often.

The importance of mental qualities

Most athletes or sportspeople are well aware of the fact that mental factors can influence performance. This influence can be negative as well as positive; in fact most people, whether they are competing or just watching sport, are probably more familiar with witnessing performance breakdowns as a result of poor mental skills than seeing successful performances where the influence of positive mental skills is perhaps not so evident. It is important to realise that this applies not just to the production of consistently high levels of performance during competition but also to the learning of new skills and the refinement of existing skills. But what exactly are these mental factors or qualities that seem to be somewhat mystical to many people? If we were to make a comparison of sportspeople who perform consistently well across a variety of sports, we would find that most competitions are won by performers who seem to share a particular set of characteristics.

Desirable mental qualities:

✔ Taking full responsibility for their own actions; accepting blame where appropriate rather than looking to apportion it elsewhere

✔ Thriving under pressure, indeed pressure brings out the best in them

✔ Being totally committed to every aspect of the programme whether it is a tough fitness regime, their diet, skills development or anything else

✔ Remaining fully focused in spite of distractions

✔ Remaining confident and positive even when things aren't going well or going to plan

✔ Having control over thoughts and emotions such as anger, frustration and anxiety

✔ Not being afraid to make mistakes. In order to achieve their ultimate moments top performers are prepared to stick their necks out and take some risks whilst attempting to strike the right balance between their need for achievement and their fear of failure

Performers that possess these qualities are said to be 'mentally tough', and it is this mental toughness that separates the winners from the also-rans.

Some of Britain's top sailors like Ben Ainslie and Iain Percy seem to possess these skills naturally and in abundance but the majority of the top names will have worked hard to develop and refine them. Your aim as a sailor is to develop a set of mental skills that will work for you, i.e. a set of skills that will enable you to be strong with regards to these primary mental qualities. The important word here is 'skills'. Mental skills, just like physical skills, have to be learnt. This means that you must be prepared to commit time and effort to learning them in the same way that you

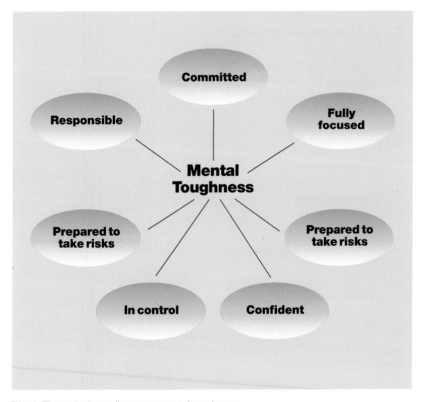

Fig 1. The typical contributors to mental toughness.

commit time and effort to improving your boat handling, boat preparation and physical fitness.

One note of caution though: sport

Opposite page: It is mental
toughness that separates winners
from the also rans

psychology isn't the missing ingredient that will suddenly turn you from a good club level sailor to an Olympic champion. It is no substitute for raw talent and you will still need well drilled physical skills and technical ability. However, sport psychology should make a difference for most sailors and will help you to move from one level to the next as you begin to build stable platforms from which to grow and develop.

There are several core mental skills that are important for developing mental toughness in sailing and each of these will be covered in a separate chapter. Each chapter provides practical tips to assist development in these key areas, and

ends with a summary of the main points discussed, together with a couple of exercises to work through. The exercises should help to reinforce the most salient points as well as providing a useful starting point for developing each of the key skills. My suggestion is that you read the whole book before you start to work on any of the specific exercises as some will probably be more appropriate for you than others. Chapter 10 provides a guide on how to put it all together, and the book finishes with some brief case studies that show how the formal introduction of sport psychology techniques made a positive difference to sailors who were experiencing genuine difficulties at the time.

Attitude and control

Attitude and control are two concepts that underpin everything discussed in this book. They are arguably the skills that will make the biggest and most immediate difference to most sailors. One characteristic of many top sports performers is their ability to pinpoint things that they can control, and to work at these, rather than concerning themselves with things that are outside their control. Examples of controllable factors in sailing include boat preparation, rig setup, sail choice, diet, fitness and attitude, with examples of uncontrollables being the weather, tide, luck, what other people do and race management. After every race, you will more than likely hear somebody blaming their poor performance on something that is uncontrollable: 'It was too patchy out there, it was a lottery' or, 'The course was rubbish'. Similarly, sailors often blame poor performances on things that they should really have under their control: 'We had the wrong rig tension for those winds' or, 'The self-bailer was leaking'. The right attitude is really all about taking full responsibility for your own actions, not apportioning blame, and making sure that you control the aspects of sailing that are controllable. In sport psychology these attributes fall under the heading of 'professionalism'.

Opposite page: Being professional is about adopting a no-blame culture

As sailors you need to adopt a professional approach, which essentially entails the identification and control of as many of the controllable variables as possible. In the first instance this may appear to be slightly at odds with what most people understand 'professional' to mean in a sporting context. Most people would probably say that a professional sportsperson is somebody that gets paid to compete at their chosen sport, and of course they would be right. However, does the fact that somebody gets paid still mean that they can sometimes be unprofessional? Or can you be professional even if you don't get paid to compete? The answer to both questions is yes. Being professional is more about having the right attitude than whether you are paid or not.

The big question here of course is what exactly is the right attitude? Choose a model professional sportsperson (they can be a sailor or from any other sport) and try to think of the qualities and characteristics that they exhibit. The list will probably include things like being determined, never gives up, doesn't argue with others, willing to learn, and so on. Effectively, all of these points can be summed up by two key characteristics. Firstly, the top professionals are prepared to accept full responsibility for their own actions and secondly, they are in control.

To help illustrate this, consider the following: at just about every regatta that I have been to, whether it is dinghies or keelboats, club racing or World Championships, I have heard sailors blaming other people or other things for their own poor performances. I often see crews and helms arguing in the dinghy park, youngsters arguing with their parents, sailors sulking or throwing tantrums, kit being neglected or not put away properly, sailors claiming that it was too shifty or too windy, it was unfair or the weather forecast was wrong. Anything that can possibly be blamed will get blamed, except for the performance of the sailors themselves. Sound familiar? It should do, we've all been there!

The idea of taking responsibility is closely linked to my second point, that of being in control. In just about every situation that you face in your life there will be some things that are outside of your control. One characteristic of high achievers, whether they are successful in sport, business, or other areas of their lives, is their ability to identify the things that they can control, and to work at these, rather than getting bogged down by worrying about things that are outside of their control.

From a sailing point of view what this means is that we shouldn't be blaming our less than desirable performances on things that are not within our control, such as other people or wind shifts, i.e. the types of things that we normally blame. If you have ended up with the wrong rig setup for the day and you can't change it, you can either complain about it for the rest of the day and allow your performance to suffer, or you can focus on something constructive. Instead of blaming something that you can do nothing about, you should be focusing on things that are within your control and are relevant and important, i.e. things that will be of benefit. The great thing about the uncontrollables is that they are the same for everybody. There is nothing you can do about them so there is no point in worrying about them! Instead, you should work at all of the aspects of your performance that you can control.

A professional approach then really means that you must take full responsibility for every aspect of your own actions, and entails the identification and control of as many of the controllable variables in your performance and preparation as possible. Examples of controllable and uncontrollable factors in sailing are given in Figure 2.

Controllables	Uncontrollables
Effort & Determination	Winning!
Your Performance	Outcome of the Event
Concentration	Weather
Goal Setting	Tide
Diet & Fitness	Condition of
Boat Preparation	the Venue
Boat Set up	Behaviour or
Boat Handling	Performance of
Dedication	Opponents
Commitment	Officials / Decisions
Time Management	Luck
Attitude to Mistakes	Illness
Attitude to Others	Accidents
Communication	Event Location
Thoughts and Emotions	
Venue Preparation	
Discipline	
Knowledge of the Rules	

Fig 2. Typical controllables and uncontrollables.

You will see that 'winning' is in the uncontrollables list. This is because there are simply too many factors outside your control that can influence whether you win or not, including how well others perform, other people's decisions, race official decisions, luck, breakages and so on. You can however control your dedication, commitment, attitude and

how much effort you put in. Provided you perform to the best of your ability on a given day you can't ask for any more. If your goal is to finish in the top ten and you finish fifteenth, you have no grounds for complaint as long as you can hold your hand up and genuinely say that you gave it your best shot and you could not have tried harder or performed any better. You just have to accept that other people were better on the day, try and learn from it and move on. On the other hand, if you finish lower than you had hoped but you haven't been professional and you haven't given it your best shot, then you have no right to complain.

The concepts of attitude and control are all about being professional by taking responsibility for your own actions and your own performance. Give yourself the best chance possible by making sure that your preparation is as near to perfect as it can be and try to adopt a 'no blame no excuse' culture that leaves you with nothing to hide behind. If you find yourself in an uncomfortable situation or a situation that seems to be causing you problems you can do one of two things: you can either change the situation or you can change your attitude towards it. If you can't change the situation then your only choice is to change your attitude. For example, imagine that you have just ended up on the wrong side of a wind shift. Your reaction might be to become annoyed, frustrated or distracted, all of which have the potential to have a negative bearing on your performance. You can't change this situation, i.e. you can't undo the wind shift, but you can adopt a different attitude that enables you to manage the situation by accepting it for what it is and acting in a way so as to minimise the loss. This would demonstrate that you are in control and that you are adopting a professional attitude.

Opposite page: You can't control the weather but you can control your boat set up

Summary

■ Understand what it means to be professional

■ Take full responsibility for your own actions and decisions

■ Control the controllables

■ Forget the uncontrollables or turn them into controllables

■ Make sure you give it your best shot

■ Prepare as best you can and adopt a no blame no excuse attitude

■ Change the situation or change your attitude

Exercise 1

Make your own list of controllables and uncontrollables

Once you have your list you can begin to work on it. You should aim to score ten out of ten on the controllables, thus maximising your chances of fulfilling your potential. Learn to forget about the uncontrollables. As I mentioned above, uncontrollables are the same for everyone and there is nothing you can do about them, so there is no point in getting hung up on them. Be honest with yourself when assessing the controllables, try not to work on more than two or three at any one time, and try to work on those that will make the biggest difference for the next training period. Over time you should work towards gaining a consistent, high level of control over all the factors that you identified as being controllable. By working on controllables in this manner you are more likely to be focused on things that are task relevant, important, and will make a positive difference. By focusing on aspects of your performance that are controllable you will also give yourself a better chance of forgetting about the uncontrollables which in turn will help to reduce anxiety and therefore help you to feel more confident – see later chapters. One note of caution: don't automatically dismiss all of the items in the uncontrollable column. You may not be able to control the weather for example but you can certainly improve your knowledge of meteorology, which will help you to understand what might happen next on the race course.

Controllables	Uncontrollables

Note: this table and the ones that follow may be photocopied for personal use.

Exercise 2

What does being professional mean to you?

Think of a sporting role model and make a list of the
qualities that they exhibit that contribute to their
'professionalism'. How many of these apply to you?

Role model:	
Professional qualities	**My qualities**

Think about what you can change in order to have a more professional attitude. Maybe you can think of some instances in the past when you haven't been professional. How might the outcomes of these instances been different had you been more professional?

Attitude and control: Stop, Start, Continue

A useful approach might be to think in terms of 'Stop, Start, Continue'. See the example in the table below, and try one for yourself.

Stop	Losing my cool when things don't go my way
Start	Trying to only focus on controllables
Continue	To work on developing a more professional attitude

Stop	
Start	
Continue	

Goals and goal setting

> Goals not only drive your programme on a day to day basis, they give you direction and confidence.

The previous chapter looked at developing a professional attitude and focused on the need to control the controllables and deal with the uncontrollables. This will have provided many of you with some target areas to work on, and may well have been your first attempt at formally setting yourself goals to work towards.

Excellence in performance begins with a vision of where you want to go and a commitment to do whatever it takes to get you there. Your dreams may be your ultimate visions, but it is effective goal setting that will help you remain committed enough to get you there. But what actually is a goal? Somebody once told me that a goal is the three bits of wood at either end of a football pitch. This might sound like a clever answer but if you think about it, if those bits of wood weren't there the game would be pretty pointless. Goals then provide us with a sense of where we are going together with some direction and control. Although modern sport science readily accepts these points they are also rather neatly highlighted by the following piece of classic nineteenth century literature:

Opposite page: Well set goals provide direction and control

'Excuse me, Sir,' Alice inquires,
'Could you tell me which road to take?'
Wisely, the caterpillar asks,
'Where are you going?'
Somewhat dismayed, Alice responds
'Oh, I don't know where I am going, Sir.'
'Well,' replied the caterpillar,
'if you don't know where you are going,
it really doesn't matter which road you take'

(from *Alice in Wonderland* by Lewis Carroll)

In other words, it is goal setting that puts you on the right road!

Before setting yourself some goals however, you need to be aware of the fact that there are different types of goals and each of them has an important part to play with regards to providing a platform for success.

Dream goals

Firstly, there is the 'dream goal' or 'moon shot'. This is the ultimate vision, winning the gold medal or becoming World Champion. This sort of goal is really out of your direct control, but nonetheless it is special, and will probably be influential in what you ultimately do. Your dream goals are what force you out of bed on cold, wet, windy winter mornings to go sailing or training rather than staying in and watching TV or hanging out with your mates. Dream goals often (though certainly not always) have their seeds sown at a relatively young age when a young performer witnesses something special that triggers thoughts and feelings like 'maybe that could be me' or 'just imagine how great that must feel'. The journey towards the dream goal is a long one but if the seeds are sown deep enough and the desires remain strong enough then there is no limit to what can be achieved.

In order for your dream to become reality the most important thing is for you to believe that it can be done. Believing in something sets the mind in motion to find a way to do it. If you really believe that you can reach your dream, and you really want it, your mind will constantly work for you to help you find ways of achieving it. You will be constantly focusing on the positive.

Outcome goals

Closely related to dream goals are 'outcome goals'. Typically these might include winning the next event or the next race. On the face of it outcome goals are intuitively the right kind of goal to have. Which competitor doesn't want to win the regatta or the next race?

The problem is that there are several inherent weaknesses with trying to perform at this 'outcome' level. If there are twenty people in the race and they each have winning the race as their goal, then nineteen people are going to fail and be disappointed. It is easy to become demoralised with this kind of goal orientation. Outcome goals are not directly within your control because there is always the possibility that uncontrollable factors (see previous chapter) such as a change in the weather, gear failure or the performance of others might come into play and subsequently influence the result. On a given day you might perform at your absolute best but that doesn't stop someone else from being better.

Being outcome oriented can also lead to inflexibility or poor adaptability where goal setting is concerned. For example, perhaps your outcome goal was to win the last race. You round the last mark in tenth place, the plan hasn't worked, there is no way you are going to win the race so you have failed to achieve your goal. Your head goes down and you finish thirteenth. However, what you don't know at the time is that had you worked really hard and gained just two places you would have won the regatta despite not achieving your outcome goal for that particular race.

Adopting an outcome orientation has some potential pitfalls. That doesn't mean that outcome goals should be entirely rejected; as with dream goals they do have an important role to play. If outcome goals are used primarily to help set longer term objectives then they can serve as useful motivators and direction-finders in the shorter term, particularly when used in conjunction with performance and process goals.

Performance goals

The third type of goals are 'performance goals'. These are specific goals or measures which may in the end produce the desired 'outcome'. In a sport such as athletics, it is easy to set performance goals. Running a personal best time for example, or throwing a javelin further than you ever have before are examples of performance goals that do not necessarily result in winning the event. They do however provide you with a useful measure or benchmark from which you can aspire to new goals. Performance goals for sailing are a little more difficult to set but might include things like getting the spinnaker up within 5 lengths of the windward mark, or hitting the start line with maximum speed within 2 seconds of the gun etc.

Process goals

The fourth type of goal really underpins performance and these are known as 'process goals'. Process goals can be thought of as the short term goals or stepping stones that you will use to help achieve the outcomes. Process goals are the 'hows' of goal setting in that outcomes are what you *want* to achieve and processes are *how* you are going to achieve them, i.e. what you are actually going to do. Process goals are very much within your control.

Typical process goals include things like focusing on the tell tales, being relaxed, sailing with a constant angle of heel, smooth steering etc. These are all things that are within your direct control, i.e. you can do something about them. In that respect they can also be thought of as being task relevant and important.

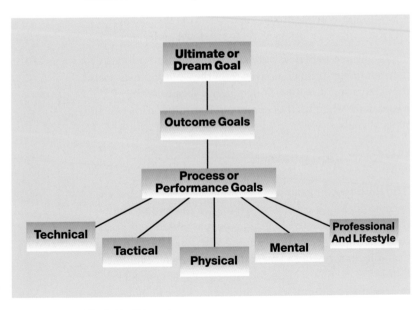

Fig 3. Goal hierarchy.

The idea is simple. By operating at the process level, the performance will take care of itself, and if the desired performances are being achieved then there is an improved chance of the outcomes happening as well. In this respect the different types of goals can be thought of as co-existing as a kind of hierarchy where success at one level improves the chances of success at the next (see Figure 3).

In the example given above, rounding the last mark in tenth place with an outcome orientation resulted in the sailor not achieving his or her outcome goal. Had that sailor adopted a process oriented approach and focused on aspects of their performance that were controllable or task relevant such as boat speed, or making sure that they were in phase with the wind shifts, they would have had a better chance of achieving a race result that was good enough to achieve the original outcome goal for the event.

The Pyramid of Excellence shown in Figure 4 is a neat illustration of how process goals can be thought of as the building blocks or stepping stones that take you towards your desired outcome. Thinking of your goals in this way highlights two important facts. Firstly, having more process goals under control means that the outcome can be higher or better, and secondly, the wider the base, the more stable the pyramid, which means that it is less likely to fall down under pressure.

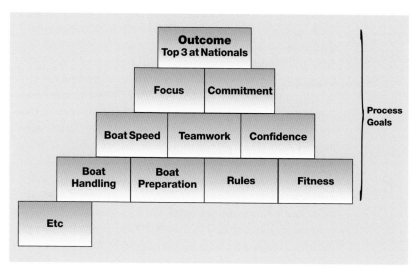

Fig 4. The Pyramid of Excellence.

Another way of thinking about process goals is to think of an individual race as a whole series of processes. For example, firstly you need a good start, then you need to look for the first shift, work the correct side of the beat, get a good lane to the windward mark, do a good mark rounding, set yourself up for the run, plan your approach to the leeward mark and so on. By thinking of task related processes you are less likely to think of previous mistakes, and won't get distracted by thinking too far ahead. If the processes are being achieved you have a better chance of achieving the outcome anyway. If you focus on the outcome to begin with you are in danger of missing important cues along the way.

Opposite page: Use process goals as the stepping stones towards achieving your outcome goals (or use 'processes' to help achieve your 'outcomes')

Having a process approach has some other useful side benefits. It can help with concentration and anxiety simply because it provides something else for you to focus on, and doesn't allow distractions to enter your head. This is discussed in more detail in later chapters.

A great sporting example of goal setting concerns an American swimmer called John Naber. At the 1972 Olympics Mark Spitz won seven gold medals with seven world records. This provided the inspiration for John to decide that he wanted a gold medal for himself and that he would get one in 1976. Already an accomplished swimmer, John worked out that he would need to improve his personal best by four seconds in order to win gold in 1976. Four seconds in swimming is monumental, it was a huge task and John initially thought that it couldn't be done. Then he started thinking. I've got four years to achieve this, four years to train and work hard. That's only one second per year. That's still a large amount. If I train ten months of the year, that's 1/10th of a second per month. That equates to 1/300th of a second per day. I swim four times a day so that is 1/1200th of a second every time I get in the pool. 1/1200th of a second is a ridiculously short space of time. All of a sudden the dream was believable. John refused to accept that he couldn't improve by that much each time he went in the pool by making slight improvements to technique, breathing, fitness, diet, attitude etc. John Naber won gold in 1976. In fact he won four!

This story highlights how important it is to set goals every day. It is a great example of using processes to achieve outcomes which in turn resulted in the dream goal, the ultimate vision. In Ben Ainslie's *Laser Campaign Manual* Ben says that he first dreamt about winning a gold medal aged about ten but he goes on to suggest that the improvements really started coming when he began to take responsibility for his own actions and began setting structured short, medium and long term goals.

For most people, identifying the goals is the easy bit, it is achieving them or making it all happen that is the hard bit. Fortunately there are a few guidelines and principles that should help.

Goal setting guidelines (how to set SMART goals)

It goes without saying that goals need to be effective, and for them to be effective they need to be challenging, positive and SMART (Specific, Measurable, Attainable, Relevant, and Time phased).

Specific

The more clearly goals are specified, the better they will guide you to your long term objective. Instead of saying that your goal is to improve your boat handling, be more specific about exactly what aspects of your boat handling need improving, e.g. roll tacking or heavy air gybing. Goals that are vague are like poor directions which make it harder to find your way.

Measurable

If you are to gain confidence from reaching your goal, you need to be able to know that you have achieved it! How will you know that you are getting better? For example, if you are working on roll tacking you might say that you will continue to tack until you have done four perfect tacks in a row before you go home or before you do something else. As this becomes easier, increase it to six tacks, or set the standards higher. Similarly you could time how long it takes to get the spinnaker filling after the windward mark, or time how long you can hold your position on an imaginary start line and so on.

Attainable

Goals should be challenging and within your control, but be realistic. Don't burden yourself with an impossible goal. If you set the bar too high you run the danger of continually failing, which can be incredibly demoralising. On the other hand, if your goals are too easy and not sufficiently challenging then motivation will suffer.

Relevant

Effective goal setting demands that you work on your weaknesses. Decide what YOU want to achieve. Do not borrow other people's goals. Make sure that the goals you have set yourself are relevant to what you are trying to achieve, i.e. that they are taking you in the right direction.

Time phased

You need to think of goals over the short, medium, and long term. By setting time limits for achieving your goals, you are more likely to make improvements.

A non-SMART goal might be something like: 'This winter I am going to work mostly on my boat handling'. In principle this is a perfectly good goal; if your boat handling improves you are likely to start getting better results. However, although this goal has been set with good intentions the fact remains that the SMART alternative has a much better chance of delivering the desired results. The SMART alternative might be something like: 'Over the next three months I am going to work on my boat handling (time phased). I will spend 1.5 hours twice a month working on specific boat handling issues including roll tacking, hoists and drops and acceleration (specific). I will set daily goals for each training session that allow me to monitor my performance and make continual progress towards being able to give myself a minimum of nine out of ten in each area on 90% of occasions (measurable and attainable – i.e. difficult but not impossible).' And of course the whole thing is relevant – improving boat handling means better performance.

Working within this SMART framework encourages you to know exactly *what* you want to achieve, *how* you are going to do it, and *when* you are going to do it. By identifying short and medium term process goals that will lead to the longer term outcome goals, you will have a clear idea of what you need to be doing every month/week/day in order for you to achieve your outcomes.

Ask yourself a series of questions such as:

✔ What do I need to have achieved in three months' time in order to be on track for my 12 month goal?
✔ What do I need to achieve this week?
✔ How am I going to do this?
✔ What am I going to do today that will take me one step closer to achieving my next goal?
✔ What have I done today that has taken me one step closer?
✔ Is what I am about to do SMART?

Other goal setting tips

Another well established fact in the world of goal setting is that the most successful people are those that write their goals down. If you want to achieve your goals write them in a diary or planner so that you get an idea of exactly when you will be doing the things that will lead to the goals you have identified.

Opposite page: Be prepared to change your goals as circumstances change

Writing them down also helps you to check on progress and helps to ensure that your goals become actions.

Goals should also be expressed as desirable or positive behaviours as opposed to negatives. In other words try to express your goals in terms or behaviour that should be exhibited rather than behaviour that should not. For example, as you approach a windy gybe mark it is far better to focus on 'staying upright' rather than 'not capsizing'. Better still, you should focus on the processes involved in staying upright such as 'pick a good wave', 'smooth tiller movements', 'positive weight transfer' and so on.

Your goals should be reviewed regularly as proper evaluation is essential. Spend a little time reflecting after every training session, race or regatta so that you know what was good and what wasn't, what worked and what didn't. This applies whether you are sailing a single handed boat or you are part of a ten man crew on a 40ft cruiser-racer. As you sail or motor out to the starting area at the beginning of the

day take some time to decide (or in a crew discuss and agree) what the objectives for the day are and how you will know when you have achieved them. On the way back or when you get ashore take some time to reflect or debrief the day. Talk about what worked and what didn't, how well the goals for the day were met, what you can implement for next time and how you can improve for next time. This helps you to carry best practices forwards and helps you to drop things that aren't a good use of your time. It also helps you to monitor progress so that you know you are on track.

One golden rule for debriefs or evaluations is to always try to end on a positive. In fact I'd suggest taking this a stage further so that you begin with a positive, then move on to any negative issues or anything that warrants constructive criticism and finally end up with a positive.

It is important to understand that the goals you set for yourself should not be cast in stone, and that they need to be flexible or dynamic. Be prepared to change them if circumstances change or if they become too easy or too difficult. If your goals are too easy then you run the risk of becoming complacent, but if they are too hard you can easily become de-motivated and fed up.

As well as guiding you towards success, there are many other benefits associated with effective goal setting, including:

✔ Improved concentration and focus. By providing you with focus they help to prevent negative or distracting thoughts from entering the mind

✔ Improved motivation and persistence. By setting short, intermediate and long term goals you establish the steps to eventual success

✔ Maximised effort put into a task. If a goal is important to you, you will generally put more effort into achieving that goal

✔ Improved confidence. By setting and achieving a series of appropriately structured goals you will build up a steady stream of positive experiences which confirm your abilities and make you feel good

✔ By improving confidence, goals will also help to reduce the negative components of anxiety

Goal setting is therefore another primary tool in the development of mental skills for sailing and has many associated benefits. It may sound like a cumbersome and drawn out process but really the whole thing is underpinned by some quite straightforward principles. Essentially goal setting allows you to make much better use of your time so that you are continually achieving. As I said at the beginning of this chapter, your dreams may be your ultimate visions, but it will be your effective goal setting that will help you to remain committed enough to get you there. Goals are essential to success – no goals means no achievement!

Summary

- Identify outcome goals but set process goals. It is important to have the right blend of both

- Set goals for practice and for competition

- Set positive goals as opposed to negative goals

- Make sure that goals are within your control. It would be better if your goal was 'to be assertive on the start line' (within your control) than 'to avoid starting in the second row' (negative and not fully within your control)

- Be SMART!

- Record and display goals once they have been identified. This is your contract with yourself, your crew, coach etc

- Evaluate your goals regularly to check on progress

- Be prepared to change your goals as circumstances change

Exercise 3

Think about a training session in the past that wasn't very productive. Maybe you just sailed around for a couple of hours, did a few tacks and gybes, practised a couple of mark roundings and then headed in. Now think about how you might plan that training session differently if you had the chance to do it again having read this chapter. How much more productive is the revised version?

Using the same goal setting principles write down some ideas for future training sessions.

Goal setting: Stop, Start, Continue

Stop	Being outcome focused whilst racing
Start	Using a more structured approach when training
Continue	Expressing goals as 'positives'

Stop	
Start	
Continue	

Opposite page: Set goals for practice and for competition

Concentration

' The ability to attend only to task relevant and important cues in the sporting environment whilst disregarding irrelevant information. '

The significance of concentration in successful sporting performance is fundamental, with many performers and players across the full spectrum of sports agreeing that the ability to direct and control one's attention is crucial to overall success. This is especially the case in sailing where the complex nature of the sport means that there are always lots of things going on around you, lots of things to think about and lots of potential distractions. Outcomes in sport are often decided by a small margin, which in many cases can be traced back to either a lapse in concentration or poor concentration in general. You have only got to read the sporting pages of the newspapers to find quotes from sportspeople who complain that their concentration let them down at a key moment or conversely that they performed well because they were very focused and didn't get distracted.

Opposite page: Concentration is not about trying really hard

But what is the difference between concentration and focus? Most of us will be able to recall many times in the past when we have been told to 'concentrate' either by coaches, teachers, parents or sailing partners. You know the scene: people with screwed up faces, furrowed brows and a really serious look trying really hard to 'concentrate'. The trouble is they don't know what they are supposed to be concentrating on. Concentration and focus are terms that are often used interchangeably, and they mean more or less the same thing, but to me, the word 'focus' implies a bit more meaning and a bit more direction. If you use the word 'focus' it is easier to direct your attention towards something specific and relevant rather than simply trying to 'concentrate'.

So concentration isn't about trying really hard. In fact concentration is sometimes described as 'a relaxed state of being alert' (in *Sporting Body Sporting Mind* by Syer and Connolly). This means that you are not thinking too hard

about too many things. You are simply focused on the right things at the right time, and are not distracted by thoughts that are not relevant, not important or uncontrollable. Concentration then is about focusing your attention on things that are relevant or important. However, knowing what to focus on and when to do it is not always straightforward, though the following model goes a long way towards providing some useful pointers.

Opposite page: Concentration is about being focused on the right things at the right time

A psychologist called Robert Nideffer proposed that concentration can be thought of as having two dimensions. These are width (broad to narrow) and direction (internal or external), and these dimensions need to be considered together as shown in Figure 5.

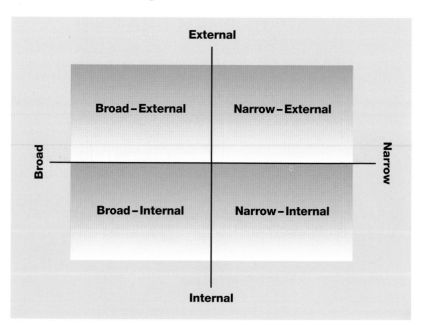

Fig 5. Nideffer's concentration quadrants.

This shows us that there are four different types of concentration, each of which is important to sailors at different times in a race.

1. Narrow external – focusing on one or two external cues, e.g. tell tales, waves, spinnaker luff etc

2. Broad external – rapidly assessing a changing situation such as a start line

3. Narrow internal – used to mentally rehearse something specific like a tack, or used to control a mental state

4. Broad internal – analyse and plan tactics or come up with a game plan or overall strategy

It is easy to find other examples to fit each of the quadrants, and it is also easy to see that you need to be in different quadrants at different times in the race. Most people will have a pre-disposition to fit into one of these groups, but in a complex sport like sailing it is important to be able to flit between them at the appropriate times in a race.

The first step towards improving your concentration is to learn about what you should be focusing on at a given time. Think about what you should be focused on at key points in the race such as the few minutes before the start, or the two minutes after the start gun, approaching a mark and so on. If you sail a two handed boat the helm and crew will have different things to focus on. For example, immediately after the start gun the helm may well be primarily concerned with boatspeed and will therefore be focused on one or two narrow external factors such as tell tales and smooth steering (or whatever other cues you favour) that contribute to boatspeed. The crew on the other hand will probably have a wider external focus and might be monitoring speed and height against other boats, looking for the first wind shift, providing the helm with useful feedback, or looking for other key competitors. As the beat develops the crew will need to start flitting into broad internal mode in order to analyse what is happening so that you can make sound tactical decisions. The options and personal preferences are limitless. The point I am making is that there is no definitive answer here but you do need to be aware of the need to have these different types of focus at different times, and you need to be aware of what works for *you*.

Nideffer's model tells us that concentration is multi-dimensional, and understanding this will certainly help you to begin to improve your ability to remain focused. The multi-dimensional nature of concentration becomes all the more important if we regard concentration as being a limited resource. This means that there is only a limited amount of it available for a given time so it is important that it is directed at the most important factors and not at irrelevant distractions. If you are distracted or focused on the wrong things then you are using up a valuable resource. In sailing this means focusing on things that are relevant and controllable such as angle of heel or smooth steering and not on uncontrollable external factors such as complaining about the weather (too light/windy/shifty etc) or internal distractions such as worrying about losing or thinking about past mistakes. The ability to sustain concentration or focus on the right cues seems to underpin consistent performance. It is a skill to be able to minimise distractions and maximise attention on relevant or critical cues. It *can* be improved with practice but as I said earlier, it is not about trying harder.

You will have noted by now that I have used the word 'distractions' many times as I have talked about concentration breaking down. That is because, putting it very simply, concentration breaks down for one reason: because you have been distracted. However, there are many different things that might distract you, and many different types of distraction!

Different types of distraction:

✔ Attending to past events: a concentration problem that plagues many sailors, young and old, experienced and inexperienced, is their inability to forget what happened earlier in a race, or even in earlier races. All too often sailors find themselves thinking about the last mark rounding, a missed shift, or a close encounter with another boat. The inappropriate internal focus on past events (usually mistakes) means that the sailor is missing all the important current cues from the environment.

✔ Attending to future events has the same potential negative consequences with the main significance of them being their irrelevance to the 'here and now'. Please note that there is a difference here between thinking slightly in the future such as planning how to approach the next windward mark, and too far in the future such as thinking about how great it will feel to win the race when you haven't even finished the first lap!

✔ Attending to too much at inappropriate times: as previously mentioned, sailing is a complicated sport and there are often a lot of things happening all at once. It is easy to try to take note of everything, although much of it may not be relevant to the performance.

✔ Paralysis by analysis: this is a phrase that is often used by sport psychologists and sportspeople alike. Sometimes sailors get stuck in an 'internal' mode for too long. It is important to understand when an internal focus is beneficial, and when it is detrimental to performance. Because sailors get 'stuck inside their head' they are no longer attending to cues from the environment, and attentional problems can occur. Another way of describing this is thinking too much about something rather than just relaxing and getting on with it.

✔ Excess anxiety: being too psyched up, too nervous or anxious will interfere with your ability to maintain good mental flexibility, i.e. you will lose the ability to flit between the quadrants as required. This means that you lose the ability to stay appropriately focused and make more mistakes as a result.

✔ Fatigue: it is often said that people that are physically fit are more likely to be mentally fit, or at least mentally sharp with regards to the demands of the particular sport. The biggest mistakes are often made towards the end of the race or regatta when tiredness is most likely to have set in. Physical fitness will help to keep you sharper for longer.

As sailors it is important to learn about the things that typically distract you. Are they external or internal (outside your head or inside your head)? Increasing your awareness of what typically distracts you means that you are in a better position to do something about it.

What can be done to improve concentration?

So far in this chapter we have established that concentration is a complex entity that is a multi-dimensional, limited resource, and is instrumental to success. Concentration fails as a result of being distracted, though distractions themselves can take many forms such as internal or external, and physical or mental. The ability to concentrate or remain appropriately focused is a skill and it can be improved with a little understanding and with practice.

The next step to improving your ability to concentrate is to develop an understanding of the kinds of things that you should be focused on in given situations, for example immediately after the start, or when faced with a light shifty breeze. You can then learn some keywords or actions to act as triggers to help you focus on the right things in the situations that you have identified. Maybe you have a tendency to not do very well when it is light and shifty. You can either think, 'Oh no I hate light air, I never do very well, it's so unfair', or you can try to turn the situation around by accepting that it is the same for everyone and identify your own performance cues for the conditions that help you to be appropriately focused, such as 'stay calm', 'head out of the boat', 'soft rig', or 'keep the boat moving'. Similarly, if it is windy, instead of allowing yourself to be distracted by worrying about capsizing at the gybe mark, identify some cues that will lead to a good gybe such as 'sail fast', 'be positive', 'smooth tiller action' etc. The idea is that these performance cues, keywords, or actions help you to be focused on the right things at the right time.

Some of you may find it easy to be focused on the right things at the right time, whereas others might need a bit more help. If you fall into the latter category then you need to begin by learning about the types of things that typically distract you, or the situations in which you find it hard to remain focused. You can do this by keeping records in a log or diary after your training sessions or races. This isn't a quick job; it will take time to build up a realistic and accurate picture.

Fortunately, once you know what your typical distractors are there are a number of refocusing strategies that you can employ. Similarly, once you have developed an idea of what you need to be focused on at particular times you can implement 'concentration cues' to help you achieve or maintain focus.

Having developed an understanding of how concentration works you can start to think about improving your own concentration skills. Read through the following list of techniques and take a little time to think about how each of them might apply to you.

Opposite page: Lapses in concentration can prove costly

Concentration can be enhanced by...

Learning about distractions. If you learn about the kinds of things that cause you problems then you are in a stronger position to do something about them. Think about instances in the past when you have become distracted or unable to focus appropriately and make a list of them. Do any patterns emerge? Do you find it difficult to remain focused mostly in light airs, or at mark roundings etc? Once you have learnt about what distracts you, you should be able to use the techniques below to help ensure that you are appropriately focused.

Identify relevant performance cues to help you to 'focus' on the right things at the right time, i.e. the most appropriate focus for the task at hand. These may be keywords such as 'smooth' or 'rhythm' or phrases such as 'head out of the boat'. You may prefer to adopt a more visual approach with the performance cues being something like 'tell tales' or 'waves'. They may even be physical such as clenching your fist or banging the side deck with your hand.

Whichever form your cues take they are used in one of two ways: firstly, they are used to refocus once you have realised that you are distracted or not in the 'here and now'; secondly, they help you to be focused on the right things from the outset. Think about how you might use performance cues in different circumstances.

Establish performance routines. In order to be consistent, or more consistently at your best, you must have a consistent base from which to perform. Routines help to provide this and form a significant part of consistent and successful skill execution. As with performance cues, routines can help focus or refocus attention. They break preparation down into a sequence of events which help you to maintain psychological control, which in turn boosts confidence and concentration, and helps to control emotions and thought processes. Many of you will be familiar with the goal kicking routine of Jonny Wilkinson, for example. Most successful sailors adopt well learnt routines that they go through every time they prepare for a race or regatta. These might include a waking up routine, a routine for rigging the boat, a routine for preparing to start or preparing to round the windward mark etc.

An example pre-start routine:

✔ 20–15 minutes to go: sail upwind to get a feel for the conditions and do some wind tracking. Come up with a basic strategy for the first beat, e.g. play the shifts on the right

✔ 5–10 minutes to go: check that the boat is set up for the conditions. Check true wind direction

✔ 10–5 minutes to go: check position of the windward mark. Is it skewed from the line? Obtain start line transits. Check line bias, which end is favoured bearing the strategy in mind?

✔ 5 minutes–start: check true wind direction if possible, confirm that the strategy is still good and position the boat accordingly

Routines help to provide security through familiarity, and help to ensure that you control all the variables that you can. They also ensure a sound focus on the right things at the right time. Not only will this benefit performance, it will also help to negate the distractions and potential negative thoughts that may otherwise invade the mind. This also helps to prevent anxiety from creeping in which in turn helps to ensure that your confidence doesn't begin to get undermined.

Opposite page: Focus on things that are important and task relevant

Develop a 'process' rather than an 'outcome' orientation. Processes are the stepping stones that help you to achieve the outcomes. They are the short term goals that help you to achieve the long term goals. For example, it is better to focus on a series of short term process goals such as correct boat setup, getting a good start, sailing in clear air, clear approach to the weather mark etc than be hung up on finishing in the top three. Maintaining a process orientation gives you a better chance of achieving your outcome

because you are more likely to be focused on things that matter, and less likely to miss important cues along the way.

Control the controllable. Make sure you are focused on things that you can control rather than things that you can't control. There is no point in getting worried about how fast somebody else is going because you can't do anything about it. It is far better to concern yourself with controllable aspects of your own performance that might help you go faster such as sail trim, smooth steering, fore and aft trim etc.

If you take the trouble to learn about concentration and how it works for you, you will be able to introduce some of these strategies into your everyday sailing programmes and be able to maintain a higher level of focus as a result.

Summary

■ Concentration is multi-dimensional

■ It is a limited resource so you need to be focused on the right things at the right time

■ Develop an understanding of what you need to focus on at different times

■ Stay in the 'here and now' and only focus on things that will actually make a positive difference

■ Don't try too hard!

Exercise 4

Try to build up a picture of how the concentration quadrants idea might work for you. When do you need to be in each of the segments? Which of the strategies described above can you use to either help get you there or help keep you in the right segment?

Exercise 5

Recall an instance from the past when you were let down by poor or inappropriate concentration. Which of the strategies could you have used to either prevent you from becoming distracted or enable you to refocus on something more task oriented?

Concentration: Stop, Start, Continue

Stop	Trying too hard
Start	Learning about what distracts me
Continue	To work at staying in the 'here and now'

Stop	
Start	
Continue	

Psyched up, psyched down, or psyched out?

I f you have taken part in any competitive sport, sailing or otherwise, the chances are you have at some point felt stressed, under pressure, anxious or just angry. In psychology speak, all of these responses broadly fall under the heading of 'arousal'. Sailing is a particularly complex and demanding sport, both physically and mentally, so it's perhaps unsurprising that we sometimes find our arousal levels getting too high, often to the point where they start adversely affecting performance.

Like concentration, arousal can also be thought of as a multi-dimensional construct in that it has both physical and mental components that combine in varying amounts at different times to create an overall emotional state of readiness or preparedness. The physical and mental components of arousal are more correctly termed 'somatic anxiety' and 'cognitive anxiety' respectively though in the interests of simplicity I will continue to call them physical and mental. Examples of physical anxiety that may be detrimental to performance include excessive feelings of butterflies in the stomach, feeling sick and needing to go to the toilet a lot, whereas detrimental levels of mental anxiety may be indicated by negative thoughts (such as 'I can't do it'), lack of self belief ('we never do very well in light airs') and poor concentration or inappropriate focus.

Opposite page: There can be a fine line between excitement and excess anxiety

For most people, it is perfectly normal to feel increased levels of arousal in certain situations. Who hasn't felt slightly nervous when rigging the boat before the first race of an important regatta, anxious when approaching a windy gybe mark, or tense when battling out a close fought race when going up the last beat? These are all normal responses and are basically your body and mind telling you that you are 'up for it', or ready to perform both mentally and physically.

The problems occur when the arousal levels get too high or remain too low. If you are too nervous, for example,

you are likely to get too tense, your movements are no longer smooth, you can't think properly and your concentration suffers. Frustration can lead to anger and inappropriate focus, and further performance decrements. I should point out at this point that for some people an angry outburst, whether it is verbal or something physical like banging the deck of the boat, can actually be a positive thing, but only if it helps them to calm down, relax, and refocus – more on that later.

The relationship between arousal and performance is complex and has been a topic for debate in mainstream psychology for the last hundred years or so. However, in its simplest form it can be graphically represented by an inverted U shaped curve (see Figure 6). The curve suggests that initially, whilst arousal is low (being psyched down), performance is relatively poor. Performance then improves as arousal increases up to an optimal level (getting psyched up), but further increases in arousal result once again in performance decrements (psyched out!). This explains why sometimes sportspeople perform badly because they are under aroused, and sometimes they perform badly because they are over aroused.

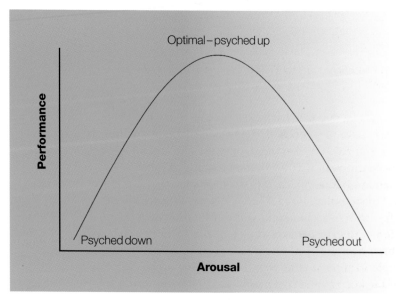

Fig 6. Inverted U performance-arousal curve.

As a sailor, your goal is to be able to reach your optimum level of arousal consistently for each race or each situation. At this point you might describe yourself as being really 'psyched' or 'psyched up'. Some people might refer to this as being in the 'zone' or 'ideal performance state'. (See Figure 7.)

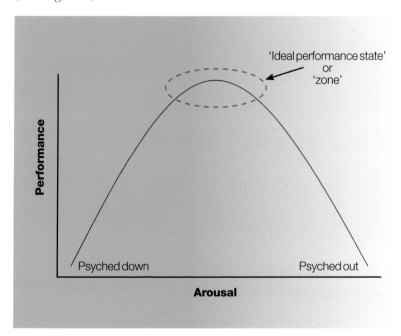

Fig 7. Performance-arousal curve showing 'ideal performance state' or 'zone'.

However, as you may have experienced, this is not always an easy state to accomplish. It is made all the more difficult when you consider that the optimal level of arousal will not only be different for each person, it will also vary from situation to situation, i.e. it is situation specific. The optimal level of arousal required when preparing to start in light shifty airs on an inland reservoir will for most people be different to that required when preparing to start in 20 knots of breeze on the open sea. It may even be different for two people within the same boat. For example, a 49er helm may need to keep a calm cool head when approaching a crowded windward mark somewhere near the port tack lay line, whilst the crew may need to be pretty pumped up for all the physical work he is about to do.

Fortunately, you can learn what your optimal arousal levels are, and you can learn some skills to help get you there in the first place, and to help stop you going 'over the top'. In other words, you can manage your levels of arousal.

In order to learn how to control your arousal levels, you will need to become aware of your feelings during practice and competition. This involves monitoring your own feelings and thoughts and recognising whether the symptoms that you experience are typically physical or mental in nature. You can then begin to learn how these are associated with your performances in differing situations. Developing an understanding of what is going on inside your head and your body and how this relates to the subsequent performance means that you are better placed to gain control over your thoughts and feelings. Once you have an idea of what levels of arousal work best for you, you can learn some techniques to help get you psyched up or down as appropriate, therefore helping you to stay at your optimal level more readily.

Dealing with over-arousal

Signs of being over-aroused include:

✔ Nausea   ✔ Feeling edgy

✔ Sweaty palms   ✔ Self doubt

✔ Butterflies   ✔ Poor concentration

✔ Needing the loo a lot

There are many ways to help combat over-arousal. However, it is important to recognise that everybody is different and what works for one person may not necessarily work for another. Similarly, different techniques may be required for different circumstances.

1. Shake out hands, shoulders and neck, gradually relaxing the muscles by shaking out the tension. Similarly, slowly stretching tight muscles is another way to loosen up any tension.

2. Use long slow exhalations. Breathing out is associated with relaxation, and inhalation with tension. Therefore, when given the opportunity during training or competition, take two or three long slow exhalations and focus on the movement of your chest. With practice, this becomes a skill that can be used readily in high pressure situations to reduce unwanted high levels of arousal.

3. Use 'cue words', often best combined with the slow exhalations to form a simple three stage refocusing technique: Breath-Talk-Action. The first stage would typically be a couple of deep slow breaths that lead to the 'talk' stage. The talk stage consists of a cue word or words, perhaps 'Calm' or 'Relax' which refer to a state of mind, or they may be something to do with sailing such as 'tell tales', 'waves' or 'spinnaker'. The cue words can be anything that helps you to refocus on an 'action', something that you can control which will make a positive difference to your sailing.

4. Use physical triggers. For some people, something simple like squeezing the tiller hard and then letting your hand relax can be an effective cue for refocusing. For others, something more animated such as banging the deck or slapping their thigh can be the cue to take stock of the situation, calm down and refocus.

5. Focus on the here and now. Thinking about what might happen in the future or what has happened in the past (bad mark rounding, or bad tack, capsize etc) usually just increases your arousal. There is nothing you can do about it anyway so get back to reality and keep your mind on the present.

6. Slow down and take your time if possible. When the pressure builds, many people have a tendency to perform too fast. Use the breathing and/or refocusing routines to help you slow down and focus on what you have to do.

7. Have fun and enjoy the situation. Most top sailors actually look forward to and even relish the pressure situations instead of fearing them. This is often regarded as being a fundamental part of developing overall mental toughness.

8. Set narrow process goals that you can control. You are better off having a few specific goals for each race (such as 'smooth steering', 'good communication', or 'maximum hiking') than having an outcome goal that you can't control, which can often lead to distraction and poor focus.

9. Have a good race plan. Being indecisive produces anxiety. One way to reduce indecisiveness is to devise a race plan and stick to it as far as possible. A good race plan removes many of the decision making situations that induce stress and anxiety and become a distraction, thus affecting concentration and performance.

10. Set up stressful situations in practice and training. A very successful way to prepare yourself for pressure situations is to occasionally practise under pressure. As you become more accustomed to sailing under these conditions, you will be less likely to be negatively affected during actual competition.

Dealing with under-arousal

We are all familiar with seeing athletes preparing themselves prior to a race, and there are certain times when you need to 'pump yourself up' or get 'psyched up' because you are feeling lethargic and under-energised.

Signs of being under-aroused include:

✔ Feeling tired or lethargic

✔ Lack of concern over how you will perform

✔ Your mind constantly wondering, easily distracted

✔ Feeling bored and uninterested

✔ Lack of enthusiasm

You need not experience all of these signs to be under-aroused. However, the more signs that you do feel, the more likely it is that you will need to do something about it. Again, there are a number of steps that you can take:

1. Positive statements. Repeat things like 'sort it out', 'I can do it', 'hang in there', 'get tough' etc, or try 'mood words' such as Strong, Tough, Aggressive, Fast, Quick etc.

2. Forceful movements. It is fairly commonplace to see athletes pumping themselves up before a competition or event and similar techniques are just as useful for sailors. Many sportspeople pump themselves up by slapping themselves, contracting and relaxing muscles (e.g. clenching fists or squeezing the tiller), jumping up and down, or maybe doing a few quick press-ups.

3. Increase breathing rate. Whereas slow deep breathing is best for relaxation, shallow quick breathing from the chest tends to activate the system and speed up the nervous system.

4. Act energised. Even though you feel lethargic, if you act energetically you will often begin to feel energetic.

5. Think of the situation as a challenge to overcome. Feel good or proud about the fact that you can get yourself

'psyched up' or into your own 'ideal performance state' before each race.

As mentioned earlier, you will need to find out what works best for you in a variety of situations. You should be aware though that all of these techniques or tools are 'skills'. This means that they have to be learned, with effort and commitment on your part, just as when learning a physical or technical skill such as refining your roll tacking or working on your spinnaker hoists. You will need to experiment to work out what works best, and this should be done during training rather than on the race course. Make sure your new skills work first in training before trying them out in low-key races or regattas before implementing them at an important regatta.

Summary

■ Arousal as an emotional state can have mental and/or physical components

■ It is normal to experience some sort of anxiety but this is harmful if it is too low or too high

■ Monitor your thoughts and feelings in order to understand what is best and gain control

Exercise 6

Think of an instance in the past when you have under-performed because you have either been 'psyched down' or 'psyched out'. Try to recall what you were thinking about and how you were feeling. How would you have liked to feel in that situation? Which of the techniques listed above could you have used to help get you into the 'psyched up' area of the curve? Repeat this exercise for other situations so that you can build up a bigger picture of what 'psyched up' means for you.

Opposite page: Can you keep a cool head when others around you are losing it?

Arousal: Stop, Start, Continue

Stop	Losing my cool
Start	Using refocusing strategies to help keep me in my ideal performance state
Continue	Using controllable process goals

Stop	
Start	
Continue	

Opposite page: Use the appropriate techniques to stay in your 'zone' or 'IPS'

Imagery

> ❝ By seeing and feeling themselves achieving their goals, imagery helps to build confidence and supports the adage that "seeing is believing." ❞

The use of imagery (others may call it 'mental rehearsal' or 'visualisation') as a mental tool should not be underestimated, as its potential value is huge. Imagery refers to either replaying episodes from the past in the mind (whether they are previous successes or failures), or creating new images in the mind (either different outcomes to events that have already happened or 'seeing' something new for the first time). For example, you might replay previous successes in your mind, along with any associated feelings, thoughts and emotions or you might try to imagine something in the future that hasn't happened yet but might happen, to see how you react to that situation. This might enable you to be better prepared when and if it does happen. The possibilities are endless. The aim of this chapter is to help you make better use of imagery by providing some guidelines to facilitate effective imagery together with an indication of how it might be of benefit.

First of all, try the following exercise (this particular one is a favourite amongst psychologists for imagery training).

Imagine a lemon . . .

Make yourself comfortable, either sitting or lying down. Close your eyes if you wish. Take a few moments to relax, maybe take a few deep slow breaths as you unwind. Now imagine that you are looking at a bowl of fruit on a table. Notice the different colours of the apples, bananas, oranges, lemons, grapes, whatever is in the bowl. Now imagine that you are picking up some of the different fruits. Note the different textures and smells. Now pick up a lemon. What does it feel like? Is it rough or smooth, cool or warm? Now dig your fingernails into the skin and begin to peel the skin off. Can you hear the lemon 'squelch' as you roughly peel it? Be aware of the aroma intensifying. Can you feel the juices on your fingers? Now imagine biting into the lemon. Does it taste bitter? Does this make your mouth water?

The point of the above exercise is that although it is a very simple example of using imagery, it uses all of the senses. This is the first rule in developing effective imagery – try to make it multi-sensory. In the same way your sailing related imagery should, where possible, use all the senses, or at least as many as possible. The more vivid you can make the imagery, the more effective it is likely to be. This is discussed in more detail later in this chapter.

Uses of imagery

Imagery can be used in a number of different ways to improve your sailing:

Confidence building – one of the things that we know about confidence is that its biggest predictor is previous success at something similar. Therefore replaying some of your previous successes in your mind in as much detail as possible is a great way of boosting your confidence because it reminds you of previous success. This is known as 'best performance imagery'. Another way of thinking about it is simply 'seeing is believing'. If you can 'see' yourself performing something successfully then you are more likely to believe that you can do it again.

Anxiety reduction – this is really the flip side of 'confidence building' in that if you focus on positive or successful outcomes you don't allow anxiety-building negative thoughts and outcomes to enter your consciousness. You can't be confident and anxious at the same time so using imagery to reinforce confidence and positive outcomes helps to prevent excess and detrimental anxiety.

Skill refinement – for example, imagine yourself performing something specific like a roll tack. What words do you say or hear that trigger the movement? Note where you are sitting, what you are holding, how your weight moves across the boat, the movement as the boat rolls upright. With practice, once you have an image in your mind you can imagine yourself doing things slightly differently, refining your technique and imagining different outcomes. Perhaps you can compare your image of yourself with an image that you have of a role model performing a similar task. What is it that they do differently that makes their execution of the task better than yours? If you are able to mentally rehearse what it would be like to perform the task differently you should find that it facilitates the learning of the actual motor skill itself when the time comes to practise it for real.

Breaking bad habits – having identified bad habits you can use imagery to visualise yourself performing the task(s) correctly or with positive outcomes, again facilitating the real life situation.

Performance evaluation – use imagery to reflect on particular performances so that you reinforce what was good and learn from whatever wasn't so good. With practice you can use imagery to 'see' different outcomes or 'what-ifs'. For example, imagine you are going upwind on a port tack. You tack just below a starboard tacker in the classic lee-bow position but slightly mistime the tack and end up getting rolled by the boat to windward, losing three other places in the process. If we are honest, it has happened to us all! Now replay the same situation in your mind but this time imagine a perfectly timed tack: the starboard tack boat can't live there and he is forced to tack away towards the unfavoured side of the course. What was different about your thinking and focus of attention on the good tack compared to the bad one? By replaying the positive outcome in your mind you will learn and give yourself a

Opposite page: Use all of your senses to make imagery as real as possible

better chance of success next time you find yourself in a similar situation.

Attentional control – by incorporating imagery into your pre-race routines you help to ensure that you are focused on things that are controllable and task relevant rather than disruptive distractions.

Imagery then, as with most mental skills, has plenty of potential uses and can be used in many different situations or circumstances. You must however be prepared to practise it and the more you practise, the more you can find what works for you. Remember to use as many senses as you can, though taste and smell might be difficult at times. Using your senses, trying to feel emotions or moods, and recalling your thoughts all contribute to the overall vividness of the image, and the more vivid the better. However, it doesn't matter how vivid your imagery is if you can't control it. What I mean by 'control' is that you have to be able to see different outcomes from what you actually experienced. For example, in the lee bow example given above, you need to have the ability to imagine yourself achieving the positive outcome having used the negative picture to identify areas for improvement. In other words you need to be able to alter and manipulate your image so that you are achieving the desired outcome. If you are unable to control the outcome then imagery may well be counter productive in that you will keep seeing or reinforcing the negative outcomes.

The final point regarding imagery concerns the perspective that you are seeing the images from. Some people see the recalled images as if they were looking through their own eyes. This is known as an internal perspective. Others see the images as if they were looking at a video recording, or through the lens of a camera. This is known as an external perspective. Neither is wrong and each seem to work equally well, but it would be a bonus if you could develop the ability to do both. Both perspectives can be used in different ways. For example, an internal perspective might help you to 'feel' certain things better and an external perspective might be particularly useful if you wanted to see an image of yourself performing a given task and comparing it to a positive role model performing the same task. It really is a case of trying different things to see what works best and gradually building them into your mental toolbox.

Summary

- Try to use all your senses

- Make your imagery as vivid as you can by including emotions, moods or thoughts where possible

- Imagery can be internal or external

- Work towards being able to manipulate the outcomes

- Consider the types and methods of imagery that will work for you

Exercise 7

Try to recreate in your mind an example of 'best performance imagery'. This might be a particularly good or successful past performance, perhaps a race that you won, an instance when your boat handling was particularly good or an occasion when you really felt 'in the zone'. Use as many senses as you can; it goes without saying that you should be able to 'see' yourself and you should at least also be able to 'hear' and 'feel' what is going on around you. What do you look like when you are sailing well? What kind of things can you hear? Maybe you can hear your helm or crew, the wind against the sails, the rigging or your bow wave. Also listen out for any 'internal' dialogues that are going on inside your head. What are you thinking? How do you actually feel? Maybe you feel calm and relaxed, excited, pumped up or in a state of 'flow'.

You could also think about the circumstances that led to
the good performance. For example, if your image is of a
race that you won you could also think about what set that
up. Was it a particularly good start? Were you and your
partner communicating in a certain way? Perhaps you just
felt 'good' from the outset. If so, why?

By improving your awareness of what your best
performances look, feel and sound like you will give
yourself a better chance of being able to recreate them again
next time you are in a similar situation. Bear in mind that
you could involve your other senses. It is possible of course
to include 'taste' and 'smell' in your picture. Maybe you can
taste the salt from the sea as you get covered in spray or
even pick up certain smells.

Imagery: Stop, Start, Continue

Stop	Replaying negative things in my mind unless I can turn them into positives
Start	Systematically practising imagery
Continue	Using different types of imagery to work out what is best for me

Stop	
Start	
Continue	

*Opposite page: Enhance your
imagery by including moods,
thoughts and emotions (or Best
performance imagery can be a
powerful and useful tool)*

Confidence

As mentioned in Chapter 3, one of the biggest predictors of success is previous success at something similar. In other words, if you have previously performed well at a particular venue, or in certain conditions, or at a particular task, there is a good chance that you will feel confident of performing well the next time you are faced with similar circumstances. However, there is more to confidence than that! What if you find yourself in an unfamiliar situation where you can't easily draw upon past experiences for help? Fortunately there are many things that you can do that will help to build confidence in the first place and secondly help to protect it from falling apart if your game doesn't go quite to plan. Many of these have been alluded to in previous chapters. The first half of this chapter will review them before moving on to look at some other ideas.

Chapter 2 talked about the need to 'control the controllables' and adopt a 'professional' outlook or attitude. By choosing to focus on controllables that are task relevant or important you know that you are working on things that are making a positive difference and moving you in the right direction, rather than getting stuck in a downward spiral of negativity that is fuelled by non-controllables and things that are not important or task relevant. Similarly Chapter 3 talked about the need to set different types of goals that enable you to monitor progress and make sure that you are moving in the right direction. Knowing that you are continually achieving and taking those small steps towards your outcome and dream goals is in itself a huge motivator and confidence builder.

Opposite page: One of the most consistent findings in sport research is the positive link between confidence and success

In Chapter 4, the importance of being appropriately focused was discussed, i.e. making sure that you are focused on the right things at the right time. Appropriate focus means that you aren't thinking about mistakes in the past, things that aren't relevant or important, or indeed any other distractors that are likely to undermine confidence.

Being in control, effective goal setting and appropriate focus all serve to enhance confidence in their own way,

though they are also to some degree all connected. For example, setting good goals means that by default you are working on controllables, and also means that you are focused on things that matter or that will make a positive difference. Done properly they will all help to build confidence whether you have specifically designed them that way or not!

Chapter 5 looked at arousal control and the need to be able to psych yourself up or down as necessary to make sure that you stay in your 'ideal performance state'. High levels of arousal are usually interpreted as excess anxiety or nervousness. Confidence can be thought of as sitting at the opposite end of a continuum with anxiety at the other end. This means that you can't be confident and excessively anxious at the same time. Therefore if you are able to stay in your ideal performance state you prevent yourself from becoming anxious at a detrimental level and therefore have a better chance of being at the confident end of the continuum.

We have established that confidence may well be a by-product of working on other areas of your mental game, but there are also a number of other ways that you can build your confidence and at the same time prevent it from being undermined by poor performances or things that are outside your control.

The power of being positive

One of the factors that characterises top performers from the also-rans is the ability to remain positive, even in the face of adversity, when things are going wrong or when the pressure is really on.

It is therefore useful to have a set of positive statements that help to get you into the right frame of mind, reinforcing your plus points, and enhancing your expectations of doing well. Creating a personalised list of positive affirmations about you and your abilities is a major step towards being able to think positively when you need to.

With that in mind, try to think about your sailing and create a series of positive statements about your performances that you can use as reminders of what your strengths are. Reading your list and reminding yourself of what you are good at will start to make you feel more positive and will help you to get into the right frame of mind for every race.

Examples of positive statements:

✔ I am physically fit and strong

✔ I am agile around the boat

✔ I am good at staying calm in crowded situations

✔ I can cope with difficult weather conditions

✔ I am confident in my boat handling

✔ I have a good knowledge of the rules

Exercise 8

Develop your own list of positive statements. Keep a copy in your kit bag so that you can read them before training sessions and races to remind you of what your strengths are. Wherever possible try to add a reason regarding why each statement is important (see example below). This helps to reinforce the benefit of the statement.

Positive Statement	Benefit
I am confident in my boat handling	Therefore I know that I can perform well in close boat-to-boat situations

Exercise 9

Personal reminder sheets

On the day of any race it is important that you stay positive and remain appropriately focused. However this is not always easy to do and your mind will sometimes begin to wander around, allowing your confidence to become undermined by all sorts of irrelevant thoughts that cause you to lose concentration and allow negativity to creep in. Another great way of fighting this is to prepare your own personal reminder sheet. These personal reminders have several clear benefits:

1. They remind you of previous good performances and encourage you to think about times when you sailed well in the past

2. They remind you of what you are good at. This reinforces your strengths and means that you are focused on good aspects of your performance

3. They remind you of what you need to concentrate on, i.e. things that are relevant and important

4. They give you appropriate things to think about during the race itself

Look at the example personal reminder sheet opposite and then complete your own sheet using the following guidelines:

• List three times when you sailed at your best

• List what was good about these performances

• List three things that you need to do in order to perform well

• Write down what you need to do to achieve these

• List your three key strengths

• Write down a phrase to get you going; a kind of contract with yourself

Example performance reminder sheet

Top performances:	What was good about them:
1. First race at the inland championships	Excellent start and read the shifts well
2. The windy race in last year's open meeting at Weymouth	I felt strong, very much in the groove and boat handling was good
3. National ranking event at Hayling Island	Stayed confident despite poor start and made a great comeback

Replay these in your mind using as much detail as you can to reinforce what you are good at.

Top three performance drivers

I need to be:	Therefore I need to:
1. Calm and relaxed	Stay in the 'here and now', use key words and thoughts
2. Positive	Use reminder sheet and positive statements
3. Well prepared	Trust my routines, adhere to race plan

My key strengths are:

1. Fitness

2. Boat handling

3. Determination

Before each race I will take a few slow deep breaths, relax, and imagine myself performing well, staying positive and never giving up.

Positive self-talk

One of the most consistent findings in sport psychology research is the direct link between confidence and success. The fact is that the top performers are generally confident people, though of course their confidence has been developed over many years and is often at least partly due to positive thinking and the many previous experiences in which they have performed well. So from a practical point of view it would appear to be fairly clear that what the top performers think or say to themselves is critical to their overall successes. If you observe the top performers in any sport you will often see that they appear to spend a lot of time 'talking' to themselves. Much of the time they may not even be aware of this internal dialogue, much less its content or what it means. However, we do know that these thoughts, whether or not they are audible or conscious, directly affect feelings and ultimately actions. In other words, what you say and what you think do make a difference. Inappropriate or negative thinking usually leads to negative feelings and poor performance, just as appropriate or positive thinking leads to positive feelings and good performance.

Having control of your thoughts is potentially of huge benefit to you in improving confidence and performance. With practice you can learn to use positive self-talk to enhance performance and replace self-defeating negative thoughts with positive ones, i.e. thoughts that build confidence and the expectation of success.

In order to use self-talk effectively you must first develop an awareness of the kinds of things that you typically say or think whilst you are sailing. You can do this by thinking about your past performances, good or bad, and making some notes. Maybe your helm or crew can help with this or you can keep a diary so that you record your thoughts as soon as possible after sailing. By building up a picture of what you typically say and think you put yourself in an informed position with regards to what might need changing. You may find that most of your self-talk is positive and not much needs changing. On the other hand you may find that you are consistently saying or thinking negative things in certain situations. For example, you might find that every time you arrive at the boat park to be greeted with light offshore winds you think something like, 'Oh no, not light shifty winds again, we never do well when it's like this, it's so unfair…'

Fortunately there are a couple of really easy techniques that you can use to turn this kind of scenario into a positive. The first is called 'thought stopping'. As soon as you have realised that your self-talk is negative you simply tell yourself to STOP and immediately switch your focus to something positive instead. Some people like to imagine seeing a red STOP sign flash up in front of them, but it really doesn't matter what. What is important is that you use this as the trigger to start doing, saying, or thinking something more constructive or positive.

A second technique is called 'countering'. This is slightly different in that in the first instance you acknowledge the cause of the problem and then turn it around into something positive. In the example given above, the counter might be something like, 'I know that it is light and shifty but it's the same for everyone, let's get the boat set up for light airs and get on the water with a light airs mentality…' (the light airs mentality being a set of key words or statements such as 'head out of the boat', 'look for the new pressure', or 'smooth movements', etc).

This approach therefore doesn't deny or downplay what you are experiencing but allows you to acknowledge what is happening in a positive manner and to your best advantage.

Exercise 10

Try to make up a list of typical thoughts and self-talk and take a look to see whether it tends to be positive or negative, helpful or destructive. Then think of how you might use either the 'thought stopping' or 'countering' techniques to help you to become more positive. With practice you could even incorporate these into your imagery so that you can imagine positive outcomes from previous situations that had begun with a negative.

This chapter has taken a look at where confidence comes from and provides some practical tips for enhancing and developing it. In addition there are some suggestions for helping to ensure that your confidence doesn't become undermined by things that are not within your control or which aren't relevant. For most performers, regardless of the sport, confidence is a valuable commodity but one which can be rather fragile. Developing a better understanding of what works for you will help to ensure that your confidence remains robust.

Summary

- Confidence is enhanced by controlling the controllables, goal setting and appropriate focus

- You can't be anxious and confident at the same time. Therefore reducing anxiety improves confidence and, likewise, improving confidence reduces anxiety

- The biggest predictor of success is prior success at something similar – develop your own reminder sheets accordingly

- Make sure that you know your strengths

- Be positive

Confidence: Stop, Start, Continue

Stop	Being negative when things start going wrong
Start	Using positive self-talk
Continue	Reinforcing my strengths

Stop	
Start	
Continue	

Opposite page: Don't underestimate the power of being positive

FOCUSed for Success

Facilitated Ongoing Conscious Understanding of Success

FOCUS is a powerful and personalised evaluative tool that helps sailors improve their self-awareness with regards to their perceived key elements of sailing. Its key strengths are its flexibility and the fact that it provides a great platform for objective and measurable goal setting and in the process takes goal setting to a higher and more detailed level.

Additional benefits of implementing FOCUS:

✔ Enhanced self-awareness

✔ Identification of strengths and weaknesses

✔ Monitoring of progress

✔ Enhanced motivation

✔ Behaviour modification

✔ Enhanced confidence

The FOCUS process begins with the sailor compiling a list of all the key elements that they regard as being contributory to success at sailing. These items are entered into the first column of the FOCUS worksheet, which you can create yourself.

Key Elements	Importance	Excellence	Actual	Discrepancy	Focus
Boat handling					
Boat preparation					
Tactical/strategic					
General skills					
Mental skills					
Fitness					
Other					

Fig 8. Example of FOCUS worksheet showing a basic list of key elements.

Some sailors prefer to work with a minimalist 'global' list such as the one shown in Figure 8, whilst others prefer a more detailed list such as Figure 9.

Key Elements	Importance	Excellence	Actual	Discrepancy	Focus
Equipment					
Hull					
Foils					
Sails					
Deck gear					
Rig tune					
Technique					
Starting					
Acceleration					
Windward marks					
Leeward marks					
Spreader legs					
Roll tacking					
Tacking					
Roll gybes					
Gybing					
Upwind flat water					

cont.

Key Elements	Importance	Excellence	Actual	Discrepancy	Focus
Upwind swell					
Upwind chop					
Downwind flat					
Downwind waves					
Kinetics					
Body position					
Tactical/ strategic					
General strategy					
Percentage sailing					
Covering					
Boat on boat					
Fleet					
Rules					
Compass work					
Tides					
Options					
General skills					
Meteorology					
Great escapes					
Protest technique					
Mental skills					
Appropriate goals					
Focus					
Relaxation					
Attitude					
Race evaluation					
Other					
Communication					
Teamwork					
Regatta lifestyle					
Nutrition					
Weight					
Fitness					
Event preparation					

Fig 9. Example of a more comprehensive FOCUS worksheet.

Once the Key Elements have been agreed by crew members and/or coaches if applicable, they should be entered into the first column of a worksheet as in Figure 9. The remaining columns are filled in as follows:

Importance. Score this column out of 10 with regards to how important each of the key elements is for the next training period (normally 3 months). A score of 10 is very important and a score of 0 is very unimportant. You might think that everything is equally important but different items will become more or less so at different points in the season. For example, at the end of the season, boat preparation is probably not very important if you are planning to do any winter training. It will be more important to have everything ready for the start of the season. On the other hand, the off-season is a good time to work on elements such as improving your rules knowledge and working on your fitness when the weather or hours of darkness might prevent you from doing much sailing.

Excellence. This represents the best score that you could ever achieve or hope to aspire to and if we lived in a perfect world would normally be 10 out of 10 on each item.

Actual. This figure is how you rate yourself at this point in time with regards to what you would need to score in order to achieve your longer term goals. Rate yourself out of 10 where 10 says that you are perfect and 0 says that you have zero knowledge or ability for that particular element.

Discrepancy. This is the difference between the scores in the **Excellence** column and the **Actual** column.

Focus. This is the sum of the score in the **Discrepancy** column multiplied by the figure in the **Importance** column.

If you sail in anything other than a single hander, the scores that you enter into the **Actual** and **Importance** columns need to be a collaborative or team decision. Discuss each item in turn so that you all agree on what the value should be. Be prepared to compromise, but make sure that you are all happy with what the value actually means.

You should now have a range of scores in the FOCUS column which range from 0 to 100. The items that score the highest are the items that are most in need of attention, i.e. these become your FOCUS for the next training period.

Key Elements	Importance	Excellence	Actual	Discrepancy	Focus
Equipment					
Hull	3	10	5	5	15
Foils	3	10	8	5	15
Technique					
Starting	4	10	8	2	8
Roll tacks	4	10	6	4	16
Tactical/ strategic					
Compass work	9	10	2	8	72
Rules	9	10	4	6	54
General skills					
Meteorology	9	10	3	7	63
Mental aspects					
Focus	3	10	8	2	6
Other					
Fitness	5	10	7	3	15

Fig 10. An example of a completed (but abbreviated) FOCUS worksheet.

There are a couple of interesting points indicated by Figure 10. Firstly let's assume that this worksheet has been completed at the end of a conventional season. That explains why the Importance scores for Hull and Foils are relatively low. If this sailor gave these items a high score now, then they would become an area of FOCUS for the current period, but there would be a good chance that they would need further attention before racing begins again at the start of the next season. Clearly it is better if these items are addressed just before the racing season begins so that the boat is in tip-top condition when it really matters most.

On the other hand, Compass Work, Rules and Meteorology have been given high scores in the **Importance** column because now is a good time to be working on them whilst there is not so much sailing going on. These Importance scores combined with the relatively low scores in the **Actual** column produce high overall scores in the FOCUS column.

Having completed the FOCUS worksheet you can easily identify the highest priority items because they have the highest score. These then become the items that you concentrate on during the subsequent training period. In other words they become your focus of attention and encourage you to set goals accordingly or at least serve as a reminder to do something about them. Please note that you shouldn't work on these at the exclusion of everything else but by focusing on the priority items you have an objective and measurable way of making progress in areas that you have identified as being important.

Figure 11 shows how you might use the output from the FOCUS worksheet to create a FOCUS summary or reminder sheet. Unfortunately, identifying your goals or priorities as shown by FOCUS is the easy bit. The more difficult bit is making it happen. The next step is to identify achievement strategies that will move your 'Actual' scores forwards to where you are aiming for. It is important that wherever possible you remember the principles discussed in the goal setting chapter when defining your achievement strategies, i.e. they should be SMART, controllable and process-oriented so that you will recognise progress and know when you have reached your target score on each item.

As you can see, the FOCUS tool is fairly simple in principle but is nonetheless very powerful and provides you with a comprehensive overview of your whole programme. It does however take a little time to set it up to begin with and you should allow a couple of hours to complete it thoroughly each time you do it. The beauty of it is that it is a completely custom tool, tailored by you for you. Once you

have your basic template you can use it over and over again, though you can continue to refine it by adding or removing key elements as appropriate. Ideally you should complete a fresh one every three months or so, at which point you can compare scores with the previous one. Hopefully you will have made progress in the key areas, which helps to make you feel good and serves as one of the major building blocks towards feeling more confident.

FOCUS Summary

Name: A Sailor   Date: 1st October   Review Date: 1st January

Top five FOCUS items:

		Current	Target
1	Compass work	2	6
2	Meteorology	3	6
3	Rules	4	8
4	Etc		
5	Etc		

Achievement strategies include:

1 Read latest tactics book, arrange dedicated coaching session, two on the water practice sessions

2 Read a good meteorology book, learn key differences between coastal and inland, seek expert advice about next year's Nationals venue

3 Read rules book, speak to coach about interpretations, review test cases

4

5

Use SMART Process goals where possible to achieve desired Outcomes. Try to ensure that methods are controllable and measurable and that you will recognise when the target Actual score has been reached.

Fig 11. FOCUS summary sheet.

Opposite page: Use clear and unambiguous achievement strategies to turn your goals into reality

Teamwork

> ❝ Teamwork is the combined effort of a group of people to achieve a common goal. ❞

Those of you that sail single handers, whether they are Optimists, Lasers or foiling Moths, may think that they don't need to read a chapter on teamwork because they don't operate within a team. That's true to some extent: those single handers don't exist within a team environment in the same way that two sailors in a 470 or 49er, three in a Yngling or 17 on an America's Cup boat do, but nonetheless everyone is likely to be part of a team somehow, so there is scope for everyone to learn and develop by having an understanding of how teams work and what contributes to good teamwork. A young Optimist sailor's team may consist of his or her parents or siblings whereas a member of the Olympic Development Laser squad might include other squad members, the coach, physiologist, and a whole host of other support staff in their team. In the world of foiling Moths huge advances have been made in a fairly short period of time, not just from a technology point of view but also in the pure mechanics of sailing the boats. These advances have been made because many of the top sailors have been prepared to work together and cooperate with each other in an effort to move the game forwards.

The suggestion therefore is that everybody is a team player at some level or other and that our ultimate moments, whether they are to do with sailing, work, or other areas of our personal lives, come from working as part of some sort of team where the combined efforts of the team members account for more than the sum of what could be achieved by the team members working as individuals. In other words, the whole is greater than the sum of the parts with the difference between the whole and the sum of the parts often being the difference between successful teams that are capable of great things and average teams that are stuck in the land of mediocre and going nowhere. This difference is the magical quality that transforms teams and is often referred to as 'synergy'.

So although this chapter may come across as being primarily concerned with the kind of teamwork that actually goes on between the various members of a boat crew, whether it's a two hander or a 40ft racing yacht, the principles remain the same and can be applied to everybody in all aspects of the sport.

What constitutes an effective team?

The quote at the beginning of this chapter goes some way towards answering this question but although it is a fairly typical definition of teamwork it really needs some elaboration. The quote suggests that a team is a group of people that are working towards a common goal. That is true, but the important thing is that the common goal is something that has been identified and agreed by the team members themselves rather than something that they have been told to achieve by a team manager, coach, senior team member or 'autocrat'. This may come as a bit of a surprise to many sailing teams out there, certainly many that I have witnessed first hand over the years, but democracy is the way forwards, particularly in today's politically correct climate. Of course agreeing what the team goals are may not be a straightforward process and it is fair to say that it will be rather easier to agree the team goals in a two man boat than on a typical 40 footer, which might have input from a dozen or so people. Nonetheless, managing this process is essential if the team is to have any chance of making real progress.

A particularly useful technique to help generate and manage team goals is using the FOCUS tool discussed in Chapter 8. Using the FOCUS tool, team members can meet regularly to identify team goals for competition and training and can monitor progress across time. If the team has agreed goals for the season (or for a given period of time) and written them down, the team members are more likely to remain committed to achieving the team goals, with additional benefits including maintenance of motivation, working to agreed standards (in training and competition), and better team spirit.

Another benefit of bringing the team together in a formal way to discuss team goals is that it also provides the platform for talking to one another in a frank, honest and open way. The ability of the team to communicate effectively with one another is instrumental to team success. However, learning to communicate effectively is not always a straightforward process; as a team becomes larger it not only becomes more difficult to communicate effectively, but it arguably also becomes more important to do so. Terry Hutchinson, skipper of the 2008 World Championship-winning TP52 *Quantum Racing*, is known to work hard at developing the right communication channels from the earliest days of a particular campaign. The language used on the boat is minimal and very disciplined with everyone aboard knowing what words are going to be used in particular situations, by whom, to whom and what they mean. There is no surplus of words, no ambiguity, just clear concise communication.

Opposite page: Teamwork begins with the identification of common, shared and agreed goals

Of course the actual words used will vary from boat to boat – there is no definitive dictionary or phrasebook. After all we are all different and will respond to different things in different ways. The point is that you will need to work out what sort of communication is right for you and your team: who says what, when they say it and who they say it to. An example might be deciding which crew member is responsible for calling the spinnaker drop as you approach the leeward mark. Clearly on a 420 or 49er it is either going to be the helm or the crew but it needs to be the same person consistently with the same words or phrases being used each time. A good example might be something like:

Helm – stand by to drop the spinnaker
Crew – OK, I'm ready
Helm – 3,2,1, drop!

A poor example might be:

Helm – stand by to drop the spinnaker
Crew – no, it's too early
Helm – an early drop will prevent us being pushed wide
Crew – a late drop means we might get an inside overlap
Helm – just get it down, now!

By this time of course it's all too late and the mark rounding
has gone well and truly pear shaped. This situation could
have been avoided if the helm and crew had an agreed and
rehearsed means of dealing with this situation, with both of
them knowing which one was going to make the call. In
other words they could have anticipated the fact that it was
going to be a busy leeward mark rounding and put the
relevant plan into place with its agreed lines of
communication, maybe something like:

   Helm – OK, possible trouble ahead, we'll do an early
   drop and focus on a tidy rounding
   Crew – I'm ready
   Helm – stand by, 3,2,1, drop!

In this example the crew is aware of the developing
situation but knows that the call will come from the helm.
This means that he can remain fully focused on his job and
therefore maximise the chances of him doing it well in the
knowledge that they will be executing a plan that they have

discussed and practised with each of them only hearing what they were expecting to hear.

The same rules apply to bigger boats with more crew members. On the 40 footer that I mentioned earlier, the bowman and helmsman may not be able to hear one another as they are at opposite ends of the boat. On this boat it might be that the tactician has decided how they will round the mark and he has communicated this in the right language to the helmsman so that he can execute the plan. The tactician will also inform the pitman or crew boss of the plan, who will filter this information and relay the relevant parts to the relevant people. The whole communication may be something like:

> Tactician to helm – we'll do an early drop with a wide approach and narrow exit
> Helm – OK
> Tactician to pit – spinnaker down port side please, early drop
> Pit – understood
> Pit to bow – set up for a port drop and stand by for my call
> Bow – understood

In this example the helmsman doesn't need to know that it's a port drop so he doesn't receive that information. Similarly the pitman doesn't need to know about a wide approach and narrow exit; all he needs to know is what side to take the spinnaker down and that it's an early drop. The bowman also doesn't need to know about the wide approach and narrow exit. He doesn't really need to know that it's an early drop. He just needs to know that it's a port side drop and to stand by. Of course the actual words or phrases will be different from boat to boat and will also be situation specific. Different people will want to hear different things, the point being that again, they have a pre-prepared plan, and the key crew members know exactly how they are going to respond depending on the nature of the communication that they receive.

In the examples that I have used above, it is apparent

that certain people have certain responsibilities in given situations. In other words they have a specific role to play. In a new team or in a group that isn't yet working together as a cohesive team, or perhaps when a team gets a new member, the roles and responsibilities of the individuals may not be that clearly defined and team members may be confused about what it is they are supposed to be doing. This confusion or lack of role clarity can lead to arguments and possible conflicts between team members, which in turn fuels poor performance. To a certain degree this is perhaps unavoidable in the kinds of circumstances that I have just mentioned; the important thing is to recognise that there is a need for greater role clarity and to be prepared to do something about it.

The allocation of roles and responsibilities needs to happen in a team environment via a democratic process that involves all the team members in open honest discussion. However, care needs to be taken to ensure that the various team members accept the roles that have been allocated to them. An individual's role may be crystal clear but if they are not happy about what they are being asked to do then problems can occur. These issues need to be resolved early in the process, either by open discussion or negotiation. Developing an understanding of each other's strengths and weaknesses can also have a huge impact on role clarity, role definition and role acceptance. Team members all being aware of each other's strengths plays a large part in fostering the overall team spirit. Everybody is different and this point must be accepted so that individual talent is recognised and integrated into the team in a way that enhances the team as a supportive unit.

There are many factors that combine to determine how effective a team is and how well it performs. From the quote at the beginning of this chapter we know that 'teamwork is the combined effort of a group of people to achieve a common goal'. A 'team' is therefore different to a 'group' in that a team *is* a group of people who are interacting with one another in order to achieve shared or agreed goals. A group however is not necessarily a team. We also know that for a team to become cohesive the team members must be able to communicate with one another in an open and honest way and they need to fully understand what their own roles and responsibilities are and how these fit in with those of their team mates. This can all be facilitated by developing an understanding of each other's strengths and weaknesses. As we have seen so far in this chapter, in performance psychology, whether it applies to sport or business, great teamwork can be thought of as being driven by three key constructs: Goals, Roles, and Communication.

A 'professional' approach to teamwork

One question that I am often asked is whether the various members of a team actually need to 'get along' together or like each other. The short answer is 'No' but there are some provisos. The first of these is to remember that everybody is an individual, everybody is different and therefore has different needs that need satisfying. Developing an understanding of what makes your team mates 'tick' is important in the same way as knowing about each other's strengths and weaknesses. People will always have differences; what is more important is that the differences are accepted for what they are and that whilst you are in sailing mode, whether that is racing, training or shore based, you are co-existing in a positive and supportive way that acknowledges each other's strengths and allows you to work together towards your shared goals in a professional manner. By maintaining a professional approach most differences or conflicts can be resolved with a better understanding of one another's needs, effective communication and the knowledge that everyone is doing their best with regards to achieving the team goals.

Sailing is a complex sport and things often go wrong. When they do go wrong it is certainly not uncommon for a shouting match to ensue, whether this is on a small dinghy or large keelboat. These breakdowns rarely achieve anything positive, in fact normally the opposite happens and performance suffers (as suggested by the inverted 'U' model in Chapter 5). One way to prevent this from happening is for the respective crew members to make an agreement amongst themselves that they won't

Opposite page: Great teamwork can be summed up by Goals, Roles, and Communication

shout at one another because they will always accept that the other person(s) is/are always doing their best. If something has gone wrong, rest assured that they are doing their best to resolve it. Of course this is rather simplistic and idealistic but once you have developed some trust and respect for each other's abilities it creates a very stable platform from which to work. Another simple idea is that you agree that any on-the-water disagreements are dealt with in the post race debrief, whether that is ashore or afloat between races. Inevitably some of these conversations won't be easy, it may not be fully possible to resolve a difference of opinion, at least not there and then, but done properly (and professionally) these conversations will often be turned into valuable positives. Even if the argument isn't resolved you have to agree that it is better for all concerned to try this after racing rather than during the race.

Although the short answer to my last question was 'No', team mates don't necessarily have to get along in order to exhibit good teamwork, the fact of the matter is that if they do get along well, whether it is just whilst sailing or socially as well, things will be a lot easier! When teams start working well together they are often referred to as having good team spirit. In sport psychology this is usually referred to as 'team cohesion' though this is actually made up of 'social cohesion' and 'task cohesion'. Social cohesion refers to how well the team members get on with each other socially, i.e. away from their sport, whilst task cohesion refers to how well the team members agree on what the goals of the team are. These could be the long term or 'outcome' goals or the 'process' goals that are designed to deliver them. Although it is possible for a team to be highly task cohesive without being very socially cohesive most programmes or interventions would be designed to develop both types of cohesion.

Towards the end of Chapter 3 (goal setting) I stressed the need for proper evaluation, whether it was after a training session, race or event. It is worth mentioning again in this chapter because if done well, evaluation can also have a significant bearing on helping a team to gel. One of the ideas that was discussed in Chapter 3 was the need to get as many of the sailing team as possible involved in the goal setting process as this encourages ownership, facilitates motivation and helps foster teamwork. In the same way, spending a little time evaluating the race or the regatta, perhaps reflecting on key moments and involving as many of the sailing team as possible in this process, will help to develop a valuable and positive team spirit. It also provides a great platform for any issues that have cropped up to be confronted, dealt with and put away so that they are not left to fester and cause problems later on.

Summary

Improving or developing teamwork is not an easy process, regardless of the number of people on the boat or involved in the team. As with all of the other mental skills in this book you will need to be prepared to commit time and effort if you are to improve. How successful the boat becomes will ultimately come down to how well the team members perform together. The team members need to accept that they are all in it together and that their various roles all overlap to some degree so that they are actually all dependent upon one another if the team is to succeed.

- Teams should set agreed and shared goals using the tools and techniques previously outlined in this book

- The team should work as a unit towards having clearly defined roles for each team member with each of these roles being accepted by the individual team members

- The team should establish clear lines of communication between the various team members

- Accept that everybody is different and develop an understanding of each other's needs, strengths and weaknesses

- Try to create an environment that allows team spirit to grow, bearing in mind social cohesion and task cohesion

Exercise 11

This exercise is aimed at helping you to develop a better understanding of your/your fellow crew member(s) strengths and weaknesses. Please note that in carrying out this exercise it is important that you agree to be honest and open with each other. This will not only be useful in this particular exercise, but in turn it will provide the basis for improving teamwork via other channels.

Begin by writing down a list of your own strengths and weaknesses before moving on to list those of your team mates. Now compare the lists: do you agree with each other? If you do, that's great and you have at the very least just done something that reinforces what you know of each other. If the lists don't agree then discuss the differences to resolve any outstanding issues, again being frank and honest. The resulting list of strengths and weaknesses can then be integrated into your goal setting; you might come up with some ideas to refine or tweak your strengths but you do need to try to improve your weaknesses because your overall results are likely to be restricted by your weaknesses, particularly if you are sailing at a regatta where you are likely to experience a range of conditions. Putting this another way, you are more likely to improve by working on your weaknesses than relying on your strengths.

Completing the exercise as described here will work well if you sail a two or three person boat but it may prove impractical to have each of ten crew members on a 40 footer compile a separate list for comparison. Instead the crew could sit down together and compile team-generated lists that can then be discussed openly. On larger boats it is often the case intentionally or otherwise that the crew may differ from one race to the next, further complicating the process. However, involving as many of the crew members as possible will go a long way towards helping the crew gel in its own right, with the subsequent list of strengths providing confidence in addition to directing the collective efforts in the strive for improvement.

SWOT analysis

You could take this a stage further and conduct a SWOT
analysis, SWOT being Strengths, Weaknesses,
Opportunities and Threats. This is a well-known tool in
occupational psychology that lends itself well to being used
in sport. The strengths and weaknesses that will have been
the result of the first part of this exercise now become
expressed as part of a 2x2 grid in the context of
opportunities and threats, see Figure 12.

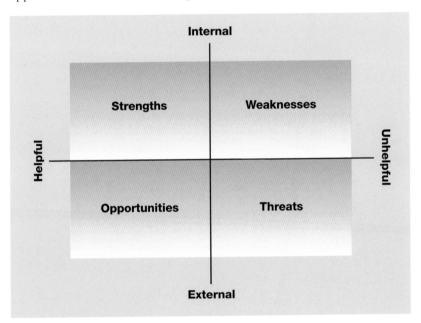

Fig 12. SWOT analysis.

Two other sets of parameters have now also been added:
Internal refers to you/your team's attributes, whereas
External refers to what these might result in, i.e. the
potential benefits that are associated with the strengths.
Similarly strengths and opportunities will generally be
helpful in that they are taking you where you want to go,
whereas weaknesses and threats are usually unhelpful. The
word 'usually' is important because in actual fact what you
have identified as a weakness might well in turn provide the
basis for some positive activity that turns a perceived

weakness into a strength. For example in Figure 13 being argumentative has been acknowledged as a weakness. However, even though this has been flagged as a weakness, it in turn becomes a positive if it leads to an activity or behaviour that improves role definition which in turn results in better performance.

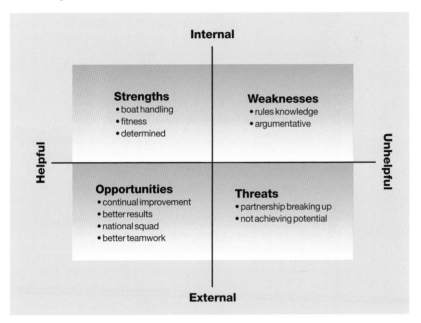

Internal

Strengths
- boat handling
- fitness
- determined

Weaknesses
- rules knowledge
- argumentative

Helpful

Unhelpful

Opportunities
- continual improvement
- better results
- national squad
- better teamwork

Threats
- partnership breaking up
- not achieving potential

External

Fig 13. Typical output from a completed SWOT analysis.

This type of SWOT analysis improves your overall awareness of your particular situation, from both positive and negative viewpoints and in doing so helps to keep your problems in perspective. In essence it will help you to identify and build upon your strengths so that you can exploit them to your advantage whilst at the same time minimising the risk of the potentially harmful effects of your weaknesses.

Opposite page: Everyone is different, use your strengths but improve your weaknesses

Exercise 12

Identifying the strengths and weaknesses of the various team members may also provide a clue as to what the various roles and responsibilities of the individual team members should be. For example, one team member in particular might have a good feel for interpreting the weather and tidal data and using this to determine the race strategy; somebody else might have a better feel for integrating this information into the upwind boat-on-boat tactics.

Alternatively it might be easier or more appropriate to begin this exercise by having the various team members 'brainstorm' all of the roles and responsibilities that they think are involved in sailing the boat and compiling these ideas into a list. There is no definitive list of items that should be included; try to include things like 'timing the start' or 'signing off' which are straightforward and need no elaboration as well as things like 'strategy' or 'mark roundings' which are a bit more involved. Once you have a list each team member should make a note of who they think is responsible for the various items. You can then compare the lists, check for areas of agreement and discuss and resolve any differences. As with the strengths and weaknesses exercise, the discussion needs to be honest and open in the knowledge that you are doing this for the benefit of the team as a whole. The resulting role clarity should help to ensure that everybody is more appropriately focused for more of the time and that team members will be increasingly aware of exactly how they fit into the team and how their individual responsibilities relate to others.

Clearly, this exercise will be easier to complete if you are sailing in a two or three person boat than a larger boat with many more crew members. Consequently, as per the previous exercise, once you have generated your list of roles and responsibilities, practicality may dictate that you discuss and assign the various roles as a team as you go along.

Please bear in mind that none of this is cast in stone; you should be prepared to modify your team's roles and responsibilities as the team develops or as team members change. The same can be said for strengths and weaknesses; be prepared to continually evaluate them as strengths are refined and weaknesses developed. As was mentioned at the beginning of this chapter, the difference between great teams and good teams often comes down to a 'magical' ingredient called synergy. This can't be bought for any sum but it can certainly be developed, enabling any team to perform above the theoretical sum of the individual parts.

Teamwork: Stop, Start, Continue

Stop	Arguing with my helm/crew
Start	Accepting that others are doing their best
Continue	To work on refining roles and responsibilities

Stop	
Start	
Continue	

Putting it all together

The aim of this book is to provide an insight into the sport psychology of sailing, regardless of whether you are a club sailor looking to climb the ranks or an Olympic aspirant. I am sure that most sailors will benefit from formally integrating psychological techniques into their programmes in addition to their physical and technical skills.

Opposite page: Consistent winners can be defined by their mental toughness

The skills and techniques outlined in this book all combine in one way or another to help create what I described in Chapter 1 as 'mental toughness', a host of qualities that are referred to as a 'whole' and which ultimately separate the winners from the also-rans. Mental toughness is difficult to define because it means different things to different people and may well change from one situation to the next. However, Figure 14 provides an indication of how the various skills might combine.

Most of the skills and techniques discussed in this book are quite straightforward in principle, but nonetheless need careful instruction and practice if they are to work effectively. The word 'skills' is important because to me it implies that they have to be learnt, i.e. you will need to be prepared to commit time and effort to learning them before they will begin to work for you. There is no quick fix in psychology; you will have to practise your new skills and be prepared to keep practising them in the same way that you will always be refining your technical and physical skills, e.g. boat handling and strength or fitness. Try to work towards a situation where working on your mental skills is a routine part of your overall training plan so that you systematically practise them several times a week. Regular practice helps to ensure that your mental skills are built on a firm foundation and means that they have a better chance of becoming second nature during competition, when you need them most.

Some of you, particularly those in full time education or employment (i.e. most of you), might at this point be wondering how you can find the time to fit dedicated

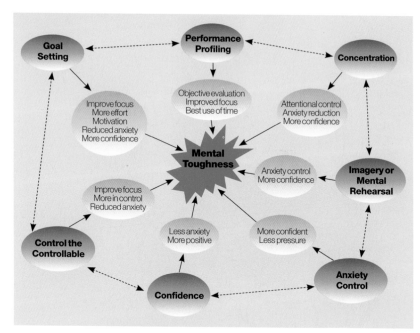

Fig 14. Illustration of how various mental skills might combine to create mental toughness. Please note that this is not definitive.

mental skills training into an already busy timetable. The first part of the solution is to accept that developing mental skills is going to be useful and valuable. Nobody got to the top of their game without having the kind of mental skills and strengths that are discussed in this book. Developing mental skills creates a valuable asset that complements your physical and technical skills and helps to make you a more rounded performer. Once you have agreed in principle that this is something that you want to do, then you can begin to work out how to slot it all in.

Planning

'Failing to plan is planning to fail.'

This is where careful planning and time management comes into play so that you can make the best use of your available time. Learning how to manage time is a crucial skill for everybody, whether it is to do with work or leisure.

Many people live their lives in a state of confusion. They know that they have lots to do but see these demands as a huge tangle of tasks. They are unable to sort out the important from the unimportant. Things may get overlooked or forgotten. Without structure, our lives end up taking the path that offers the least amount of resistance and we end up doing the simple or easy things first rather than the most important things. Careful planning allows us to be more efficient with our time so that we can more effectively prioritise our needs. This in turn leads to a clearer overview of our life and a sense of having more control. There are a number of measures that you can take that will help you make the best use of your time.

Firstly, you can prioritise. This might sound a bit obvious but there is one big potential pitfall that you need to be aware of when trying to prioritise a list of things to do. There are often too many things that need to be done, i.e. the list is too long. Prioritising a list that is too big means that some things don't get done properly whilst others may get allocated more time than they deserve. Be ready to cut things out completely if they are not essential or are not taking you where you want to go.

Secondly, you can simply say 'No' to low value activities and therefore not add to the list of things that you are currently trying to do. Before taking something else on ask yourself 'what else am I doing at the moment that has less value than this?' If you take something on and add it to the list then something else must go.

Thirdly, you can understand the difference between 'important' and 'urgent'. Any tasks can be classified as either important or urgent, or some combination of those. Urgent tasks are things like the phone ringing, or talking to someone who calls round. Important tasks are things like passing exams or getting fit. Important *and* urgent tasks are things like rescuing someone who has fallen in the water.

Simplistically most tasks will fall into one of four quadrants (see Figure 15). Some people love the adrenaline of firefighting, and revel in tasks which demand a great deal from them. They spend their time dealing with important and urgent tasks. People like this are heading for burnout. Timewasters are pottering about without accepting or

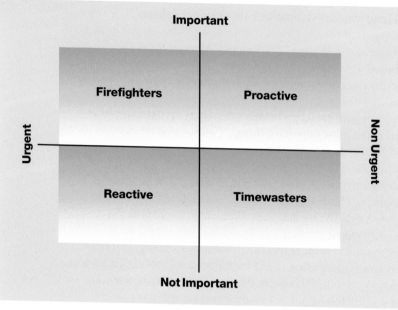

Fig 15. Illustration of the difference between important and urgent.

wanting challenges in their lives, sticking to non-important non-urgent tasks.

Many people are driven by a sense of urgency, and are very reactive. These people are dictated to by events around them and as a result often achieve very little while doing a lot. The fourth group are proactive, who consider importance above urgency. These people get things done. They try to minimise the effects of urgency by exercising as much control over their lives as possible. These people are effective time managers.

Which category do you fall into? The reality is that you probably fit into all of them at different times. The important thing is that you are aware of the different boxes. If you plan your time properly, you will find that you can shift from where you are into the proactive quadrant as you need it.

Once you have got to grips with these principles you can start planning your time more effectively. This leads us neatly back to Chapter 3 (Goal setting) and Chapter 8 (FOCUSed for success) where there are clear overlaps with this planning stage.

How do I know what to do and when?

As we saw in Chapter 3 it is important to have the right blend of outcome and process goals and to use SMART principles to drive these, but what isn't quite so straightforward is planning everything so that it all happens with minimal fuss and maximum use of available time and resources. Goal setting is pretty meaningless unless you have the ability to make it all work. One of the characteristics of successful people, whether in sport or in business, is their ability to plan everything in meticulous detail so that nothing is left to chance. They know what they have to do, when they have to do it, and how they are going to do it.

One of the principles that was discussed was the need to write your goals down. If you want to achieve your goals you need to transfer them to your diary (or whatever your preferred scheduler is) so that you get an idea of exactly when you will be doing the things that will lead to the goals that you have identified. This helps you to check on progress and helps to ensure that your goals become actions by making sure that you are working on the right things at the right time. What you are ultimately trying to achieve is a situation where your goals are driving your diary entries, and not vice versa.

Things you should bear in mind when using your diary:

✔ It is just a tool, not a way of life

✔ There is no single correct way to use it

✔ Used properly it will help you to gain control, but not over every waking second

✔ Allow for the unexpected

✔ Don't forget family, friends, leisure time, education etc etc

Where should I start?

If you start to introduce sport psychology techniques into your programme you should remember that everyone is different and hence any programme should be tailored to meet your needs. Although I would recommend reading this book completely before you begin to implement any of it, I certainly don't recommend that you then go back to Chapter 2 and begin systematically working your way through the book. For many sailors with no exposure to sport psychology at all, Chapter 2 is a good place to start but that certainly won't be the case for everyone. Some of you may know intuitively that the concentration exercises in Chapter 4 will offer you the most benefit in the short term. Others may find that the goal setting exercises or completing a FOCUS sheet tell you where to begin. If you are still unsure then you could try completing a FOCUS sheet as follows:

Opposite page: Successful performers know what they have to do, when they have to do it and how they are going to do it

Key Elements	Importance	Excellence	Actual	Discrepancy	Focus
Attitude & control					
Goal setting					
Concentration					
Arousal control					
Imagery					
Confidence					
Etc					

Fig 16. FOCUS worksheet with key mental skills areas.

Don't feel that you have to attempt all aspects of the programme. Build one skill gradually upon another. Also, just like physical skills, you should remember that the last skill that you learnt will be the first to break down under pressure. Therefore, gradually put yourself into situations that generate more and more pressure. When you are happy that you can cope at one level then move on to the next higher pressure situation. Start off by introducing the techniques that you have learnt into training sessions and gradually introduce them into competitions. Not everything will work for everyone. Be prepared to try different things and if something isn't working, try something else or try a slightly different angle. If you are unsure about where to start, the FOCUS tool will help you to identify your strengths and weaknesses and thus help to ensure that you are making the best use of your time.

Essentially, this book will provide you with a set of tools with which you must learn to help yourself. It doesn't guarantee improved performance, but it will lead to improved awareness of yourself, other people (your crew, fellow competitors, support staff), and even improved awareness of your boat, and it is this improved awareness which usually leads to more consistent performance, which in turn should lead to better performance.

Case studies

The following case studies are brief accounts of real life interventions with talented young sailors who were all experiencing difficulties of one sort or another. In the interests of confidentiality their names have been changed but the situations depicted are genuine accounts of what happened. I have deliberately kept these accounts brief, and as with the rest of this book I have kept psycho-jargon to a minimum in an attempt to draw attention to the points that really matter. The downside to this minimal approach is that it perhaps disguises the amount of time and effort that was involved in each case, both on my part and the sailors themselves, and in doing so runs the risk of over-simplifying what were real problems for the sailors concerned.

What should be remembered is that sport psychology interventions are personal in nature and should be tailored to the specific needs of the individual or team. In that respect what worked for these particular sailors might not necessarily be the answer for someone else experiencing similar issues. Nonetheless, these brief case studies should provide a useful insight into how sport psychology works in real situations, and the techniques used have the potential to be of value to anyone, regardless of the class that they are sailing or the level that they are currently competing at.

Confidence

James is a 20-year-old male sailor who has competed successfully at national level finishing in the top five at several national championships. He recently began to sail a Laser which is a more technical and physically demanding boat than he sailed before, and this initially led to what he described as being some confidence issues which were thought to be adversely affecting performance. His aim for his first year in the class was to compete on the Laser circuit and attend the World qualifiers, with the end of season goal being to finish in the top fifteen on the season's ladder.

James felt that the single biggest hurdle that he needed to overcome was that he wasn't assertive enough at starts, mark roundings and other close boat-to-boat situations, often letting other boats get the better of him when they shouldn't. This was attributed to the fact that he was unsure of whether something was going to work or not. In other words he was frightened of the consequences of getting something wrong or executing a particular task poorly, e.g. a lee bow tack or being able to hold a lane off of the start line. Secondly, he was sometimes reluctant to shout at other boats in close boat-to-boat situations in order to assert himself appropriately with regards to the racing rules, e.g. calling for water at a mark or when trying to create space for himself on the start line. This hadn't happened in the previous classes that he sailed. The subsequent conversations with James led us to conclude that most of the negative issues that he was experiencing could indeed be summed up by a lack of confidence in the new boat and his ability to sail it.

A number of possible interventions were discussed with James over the course of two or three meetings. In the first instance it was felt that imagery, used in a couple of slightly different ways, would be a useful starting point in helping him to feel more confident. Firstly 'best performance imagery' would help him to replay instances from the past when he had performed well and asserted himself well, and secondly, he could use imagery to help him rehearse tactical situations that he was likely to experience in the new boat in which he would need to be more assertive. James fully acknowledged and accepted the potential of using imagery as a means of enhancing confidence and between us we created some imagery scripts to help introduce imagery to his programme. James was also encouraged to write down a list of phrases or words that he might want to use in the situations that he had identified, with a view to integrating these into the imagery before trying them for real on the water.

Over the next couple of months James continued to use the best performance imagery to reaffirm his abilities and practise what he would say in given situations. These were rehearsed initially whilst he was sitting at home but were introduced into his training programme over the winter period together with some relatively low-key club racing.

James also created a personal reminder sheet that he looked at before going afloat. This reminded him of some of his strengths (determination, tactics and preparation) as well as reminding him of some pre-identified performance cues such as 'head out of the boat' which helped to make sure that he was suitably aware of what was happening around him in the pre-start and 'pump it up' which helped him to feel aggressive to challenge any boats around him that might be a problem.

By the start of the following season James reported that he generally felt more confident with his ability to sail the boat and deal with close boat-to-boat situations. At the early season regattas James still struggled at times but he was encouraged to stick with it and continue to refine his new skills. As the season progressed James's results gradually improved and with a lot of hard work and effort (including working on his mental skills) he eventually achieved his season's goal, finishing in the top fifteen.

Goal setting

Simon and Charlie had sailed together for about three years, firstly in Mirrors and then in a 420. They had made steady progress through the RYA squad system and were usually amongst the front runners at most of the events that they competed in.

At our first meeting they talked about a regatta that they had competed in that had not gone to plan. The subsequent conversation revealed that immediately prior to the regatta they felt that they were in a position to win the event given their good results in the previous couple of regattas that they had competed in. However, poor results in the first two races effectively ruled them out. Further questioning revealed that at the beginning of the regatta they had been focusing on the end result, i.e. winning. Simon in particular also commented that he felt nervous before the regatta started and they both felt that this was interfering with their preparation and decision making. When it became clear that they were not going to achieve their pre-regatta goal they inadvertently changed their focus to what in goal

Opposite page: Goal setting can lead to improved focus and a more organised approach

setting terms would be described as a more process oriented approach. They then went on to achieve some good results, and a respectable finishing position given the poor start.

Simon and Charlie had no real practical knowledge of goal setting and although they were familiar with some of the basic ideas they were unaware of the differences between outcome goals and process goals. Over the next couple of sessions they became more familiar with the different goal types and these were then discussed, with particular reference to the aforementioned regatta in which they felt they had under performed. The pair were able to identify that at the beginning of the regatta they had been in an 'outcome' mode and were pre-occupied with winning. Once they were in a position where they could no longer win, the pressure was off, and they slipped into a 'process' mode and began to perform better. In this process mode they were much more able to adopt a 'one race at a time' attitude, but more importantly were focused on aspects of their performance that they could control such as getting a good start, not worrying about other boats and sailing in good lanes.

With a better understanding of the different types of goals they were then able to recall previous races and regattas when they had been in either process or outcome mode, together with respective results. What became clear was that they seemed to perform better at the less important regattas when they didn't feel under any kind of pressure. This was accompanied not so much by a process orientation but a lack of a clear outcome. In other words they seemed to perform better when they didn't have a particular outcome in mind. Simon and Charlie were then able to use the knowledge gained through retrospective recall (i.e. thinking about the past) to come up with a list of typical process goals that they thought would work for them, both before and during the regatta. Pre-regatta process goals included a more structured approach to regatta preparation such as gathering weather information and any knowledge that they could find about the venue itself, for example tidal data and geographical effects. Process goals whilst racing included 'head out of the boat' and 'minimal rudder movements' for light airs and 'constant angle of heel' and 'positive steering' when it was breezy. These were practised and refined over the course of the season.

Another observation that became evident as a result of the retrospective recall was that Simon reported that at the low key events he didn't feel anything like as nervous as he sometimes did at the more important events. After further discussion and exploration Simon and Charlie began to see that there appeared to be a relationship between having an outcome goal orientation and the excess anxiety that Simon occasionally experienced. Since the issues relating to goal orientation were already being addressed it was agreed that at this stage nothing additional would be tried to directly address the anxiety issues, as the adoption of a process orientation should in any case help him to focus on positive aspects of his sailing that were controllable and task relevant, which in turn should help to ensure that his anxiety levels or nerves didn't get too high.

Over the course of the next season Simon and Charlie's results became more consistent and they eventually became an established pairing in the national squad. This success was largely attributed to having a more organised approach through a better understanding of goal setting together with the additional benefits of better focus and reduced anxiety. This is a great example of using process goals to achieve longer term outcome goals. Outcome goals are of course very important but they stand a better chance of being achieved if they are underpinned by well thought out process goals.

Concentration

Sarah was a 22-year-old female sailor who had achieved regatta successes at the highest international levels but on her own admission had experienced attentional problems in the past which she felt had adversely affected her performance. Having acknowledged this as a potential weakness she was keen to explore the use of sport psychology to help develop a set of mental skills that would enable her to deal more effectively with similar situations in the future.

The initial analysis revealed that Sarah had experienced a few instances in the past when she had got frustrated because she was performing poorly and that this frustration

led to her performing worse still. She felt that the reason for
her performing poorly in the first place was because she had
become distracted and wasn't able to concentrate
effectively. (She also felt that at times excessively high
levels of arousal had also led to inappropriate focus causing
poor performance.)

Sarah was asked to spend some time thinking about
specific instances from the past when she felt that poor focus
had let her down and to record her thoughts and feelings as
best as she could. This exercise improved her awareness of
problem situations, which in turn led to the implementation
of several strategies aimed at helping her develop mental
skills that would help her to avoid becoming distracted in the
first place and also help her to regain her focus if she felt that
she had become distracted at any time.

One of the main areas that Sarah had identified as being
problematical was sailing in light or patchy conditions. She
knew that she had the ability to be competitive in these
conditions because she had a track record of doing so.
Unfortunately she also identified that if she was going to

have a 'shocker' it was most likely to be in those conditions. She felt that this wasn't a confidence issue because she knew that she had the ability. It was more a case that when she started to lose it she quickly ended up in a downward spiral which she could rarely recover from.

Sarah was asked to come up with some concentration cues or keywords/phrases that represented what she thought she should be focused on or how she wanted to feel for optimal performance at key moments in these conditions. These included emotions such as 'relax' or 'stay calm' that were accompanied by a couple of deep breaths to help keep her where she wanted to be, as well as instructions such as 'just sail fast' or 'stay in the pressure'.

These kinds of concentration cues used in this manner helped Sarah focus on the right things at the right time, i.e. they helped to ensure that she remained in the 'here and now' and was focused on things that she knew were central to the successful execution of particular tasks. In doing so they helped to prevent potentially negative distractions from entering her mind in the first place.

Sometimes, however, negativity or inappropriate thoughts creep in regardless and once again the sports performer becomes distracted. In Sarah's case this sometimes happened before the start when she might think something like, 'I really don't fancy this today, I've just got one of those feelings' or perhaps during a race when things weren't going so well she would think, 'Maybe this just isn't going to be my day, everything I do seems to be wrong...' To begin with Sarah was encouraged to use 'thought stopping' as a means to combat these negative thoughts. As soon as she recognised the negative thought she told herself to 'Stop' and used this as the trigger to refocus on something that was more task relevant; perhaps one of the concentration cues discussed above. This didn't always work however; for many people the appeal of the thought stopping technique is its simplicity but Sarah sometimes felt that she needed more.

To that end an additional technique was introduced that allowed Sarah to acknowledge the negativity but then restructure it into something altogether more positive. For

Opposite page: Concentration cues are a great way to stay in the 'here and now'

example 'I really don't fancy this today, I've just got one of those feelings' might be restructured as 'You might not fancy this today but you know you have the ability; it's the same for everyone, set the boat up for the conditions, relax and refocus.'

The ability to identify negative or inappropriate self-statements and restructure them in a more appropriate manner is an important psychological skill that not only stops the negativity but in addition provides encouragement and support as well as redirecting attention. For Sarah, none of these techniques seemed to work in isolation. However, although they didn't work every single time, she seemed more secure in the knowledge that she had a range of refocusing skills to fall back on and she felt encouraged enough to make mental skills training an integral part of her preparation.

To find out more...

Most sport psychologists can give lectures or run workshops for teams and clubs, as well as being able to provide more specialised one-to-one help where needed.

If you would like to work with a sport psychologist it is highly recommended that you only use somebody with the appropriate qualifications and experience. In the first instance you should contact either the British Psychological Society (BPS) or the British Association of Sport and Exercise Sciences (BASES). Both organisations can provide lists of suitably accredited psychologists in your local area.

The British Psychological Society
St Andrews House
48 Princess Road East
Leicester LE1 7DR
Tel: +44 (0)116 254 9568
E-mail: enquiries@bps.org.uk
Website: www.bps.org.uk

The British Association of Sport and Exercise Sciences
Leeds Metropolitan University
Carnegie Faculty of Sport & Education
Fairfax Hall
Headingly Campus
Leeds
LS6 3QS
Tel: +44 (0)113 812 6162
Website: www.bases.org.uk

Index